Peaceful Coexistence

Mastering the Skill of Dealing with Difficult People

Alex Rivera

Table of Contents

INTRODUCTION

In our journey through life, we encounter a diverse tapestry of individuals, each with their own unique perspectives, personalities, and quirks. While many of these encounters are pleasant and enriching, there are moments when we find ourselves facing the challenging task of dealing with difficult people. Whether it's a confrontational colleague, a passive-aggressive friend, a narcissistic family member, or a manipulative acquaintance, these interactions can be emotionally draining and disruptive to our well-being.

"Peaceful Coexistence: Mastering the Skill of Dealing with Difficult People" is your guide to navigating the intricate web of human relationships with grace, empathy, and resilience. This book is a roadmap for not only surviving but thriving in the company of those who present unique challenges.

In the following chapters, we will embark on a transformative adventure that delves deep into the art of understanding difficult personalities, mastering the delicate dance of effective communication, and developing powerful conflict resolution skills. You will discover how self-awareness, emotional intelligence, and the establishment of healthy boundaries can pave the way for harmonious interactions. Through real-life examples, practical exercises, and proven strategies, you will learn to transform challenging encounters into opportunities for personal growth.

Join me on this enlightening voyage as we explore the intricate dynamics of human relationships and uncover the secrets to peaceful coexistence. Let's embark on a journey towards greater understanding, empathy, and mastery in dealing with difficult people, enriching our lives and the lives of those around us in the process.

CHAPTER I

Understanding Difficult People

Defining difficult people

Human interactions are a fundamental aspect of our lives and often form the basis of our personal and professional relationships. While many of these interactions are harmonious and enriching, there are instances where we encounter individuals who prove challenging to deal with. These individuals are commonly referred to as "difficult people." Understanding and defining difficult people is a critical first step in effectively navigating the intricacies of human relationships.

Difficult people come in various forms and exhibit various behaviors and characteristics. One of the key aspects of defining difficult people is recognizing that these individuals may not necessarily be inherently bad or malicious. Instead, they often possess traits or behaviors that clash with our own preferences, values, or expectations. It's important to emphasize that labeling someone as "difficult" should not be done lightly; it is a subjective judgment that based on the context of the interaction and its impact on individuals involved.

One common category of difficult people includes those who display aggressive behavior. These individuals tend to be confrontational and argumentative and may resort to intimidation or hostility when faced with disagreement or conflict. Their aggressive tendencies can make interactions with them highly stressful and emotionally draining. Understanding that aggression can be a defense mechanism or a result of personal frustrations is crucial in dealing with such individuals.

On the opposite end of the spectrum, there are passive-aggressive individuals. Defining passive-aggressive behavior involves recognizing the subtle and indirect ways in which these individuals express their resistance or resentment. They may appear compliant on the surface but engage in behaviors such as sarcasm, procrastination, or deliberately failing to fulfill commitments. Dealing with passive-aggressive people can be perplexing, as their indirect approach can make it challenging to address underlying issues.

Another category of difficult people includes those with narcissistic tendencies. These individuals often display an inflated sense of self-importance, a lack of empathy, as well as a constant need for admiration. Defining narcissistic behavior involves recognizing their tendency to manipulate situations to meet their own needs and the difficulty they have in acknowledging the perspectives or feelings of others. Interactions with narcissists can be exhausting, as they may constantly seek validation and be insensitive to the needs of those around them.

Manipulative people are another group within the spectrum of difficult individuals. Defining manipulative behavior involves understanding how these individuals use tactics such as guilt-tripping, deceit, or emotional blackmail to control or influence others. They may have a talent for making others feel responsible for their actions or decisions. Dealing with manipulative individuals requires keen awareness and assertiveness to maintain personal boundaries.

Sometimes, difficult people may exhibit a toxic presence in our lives. These individuals consistently engage in harmful or destructive behaviors that negatively impact the well-being of those around them. Defining toxic individuals involves recognizing patterns of behavior that consistently erode trust, peace, and harmony. It's crucial to address and limit interactions with toxic individuals to protect one's mental and emotional health.

While these categories provide a framework for defining difficult people, it's essential to remember that individuals are complex, and their behaviors may not neatly fit into one category. Furthermore, an individual's behavior can vary depending on the context and the people they are interacting with. Someone can display difficult traits in certain situations while being pleasant in others.

It's also important to acknowledge that everyone has their moments of difficulty. None of us are immune to occasionally exhibiting behaviors that others might find challenging to deal with. Recognizing this universal aspect of human nature can foster empathy and humility in our interactions with others, as we understand that we, too, can be the "difficult person" in someone else's story.

Defining difficult people is not just about categorizing behaviors but also about recognizing the underlying factors contributing to these behaviors. Difficulties in an individual's past, unresolved emotional issues, or ongoing life stressors can all shape their behavior. Therefore, when defining difficult people, it's valuable to approach the situation with a degree of compassion and a willingness to understand the root causes of their actions.

In conclusion, defining difficult people is a complex and subjective endeavor. It involves recognizing a range of behaviors, from aggression to passive-aggression, narcissism to manipulation, and even toxicity. However, it's essential to approach this definition with empathy and understand that individuals can exhibit these traits for various reasons, often related to their life experiences and challenges. By gaining a nuanced understanding of difficult people, we can better navigate the intricacies of human relationships, finding ways to communicate effectively, set boundaries, and foster personal growth in ourselves and others.

Different types of difficult personalities

Human relationships are a tapestry of personalities, each contributing a unique thread to the intricate weave of our social interactions. While many individuals enhance our lives with their warmth and compatibility, there are others who present unique challenges due to their difficult personalities. Understanding and categorizing these different types of difficult personalities is essential for effectively navigating the complexities of human relationships.

One common category of difficult personalities comprises those who exhibit aggressive behavior. These individuals are often characterized by their confrontational and hostile demeanor. They may not shy away from conflict, and their interactions can be marked by assertiveness, sometimes bordering on intimidation. It is important to note that aggression in difficult personalities can stem from various sources. For some, it may be a learned coping mechanism from past experiences, while for others, it could be an expression of deep-seated frustrations. Dealing with aggressive individuals requires patience and the ability to address issues assertively while remaining calm in the face of their hostility.

On the opposite end of the spectrum are passive-aggressive personalities. These individuals present a challenging puzzle as they express their resistance or resentment indirectly. They may appear compliant on the surface, but their actions often reveal their underlying resistance. Passive-aggressive behavior can manifest subtly, such as sarcasm, procrastination, or deliberately failing to fulfill commitments. It can be perplexing to deal with such individuals, as their indirect approach can make it challenging to address underlying issues. Effective communication and assertiveness are essential when navigating interactions with passive-aggressive personalities.

Narcissistic personalities represent another category of difficult individuals. These individuals often exhibit an inflated sense of self-importance, a constant need for admiration, and a lack of empathy for others. They tend to view themselves as superior and may expect special treatment or attention. Dealing with narcissistic personalities can be challenging because they often prioritize their own needs and desires above those of others. Understanding the roots of their behavior, which may include deep insecurities or past experiences, is crucial when engaging with them. Setting clear boundaries and maintaining a balance between assertiveness and empathy is key when dealing with narcissists.

Manipulative personalities are skilled in the art of control and persuasion. They use tactics such as guilt-tripping, deceit, or emotional blackmail to achieve their goals and influence those around them. Dealing with manipulative individuals can be tricky, as they have a knack for making others feel responsible for their actions or decisions. Their manipulation can erode trust and leave individuals feeling emotionally drained. Recognizing manipulative behavior early and assertively establishing boundaries to protect one's emotional well-being is essential.

In some cases, individuals may exhibit toxic personalities, representing a category of difficult personalities that consistently engage in harmful or destructive behaviors. These behaviors can include lying, manipulation, deceit, and a disregard for the well-being of others. Interactions with toxic individuals often result in emotional turmoil and strained relationships. It is crucial to recognize patterns of toxicity and take steps to limit or remove such individuals from one's life to safeguard mental and emotional health.

While these categories provide a framework for understanding different types of difficult personalities, it is essential to keep in mind that individuals are complex and multifaceted. Someone can display traits from multiple categories, or their behavior can vary depending on the interaction context. Moreover, individuals can change and evolve over time, which may lead them to outgrow or modify their difficult tendencies.

It is also important to acknowledge that everyone has their moments of difficulty. None of us are immune to occasionally exhibiting behaviors that others might find challenging to deal with. Recognizing this universal aspect of human nature can foster empathy and an understanding in our interactions with others, as we understand that we, too, can be the "difficult person" in someone else's story.

Furthermore, when dealing with different types of difficult personalities, it is beneficial to approach the situation with a degree of compassion. Understanding that these individuals may have their own struggles, past traumas, or insecurities can soften our judgments and enable us to approach them with empathy and patience. Difficult behaviors may be a defense mechanism or a result of unresolved issues, and by addressing these underlying factors, individuals can potentially grow and change.

In conclusion, different types of difficult personalities add complexity to our social interactions. Recognizing and understanding these personalities, whether they exhibit aggressive, passive-aggressive, narcissistic, manipulative, or toxic traits, is a crucial step in effectively navigating human relationships. It is important to approach these individuals with empathy, patience, and assertiveness, recognizing that personal growth and change are possible. By developing the skills to address and manage difficult personalities, we can foster healthier, more harmonious relationships and develop a more compassionate and understanding world.

The impact of difficult people on your life

Human interactions form the foundation of our personal and professional lives, enriching our experiences and shaping our identities. While many of these interactions are harmonious and uplifting, there are moments when we encounter individuals who present unique challenges due to their difficult personalities. The impact of difficult people on our lives is profound and far-reaching, touching upon our emotional well-being, relationships, and even our overall quality of life.

One of the most immediate and noticeable impacts of difficult people is on our emotional well-being. Interacting with individuals who exhibit traits such as aggression, passive-aggression, narcissism, manipulation, or toxicity can take a toll on our mental as well as emotional health. These interactions often evoke negative emotions such as anger, frustration, anxiety, and even sadness. The constant need to navigate difficult personalities can lead to emotional exhaustion, leaving us drained and mentally fatigued.

Furthermore, the emotional impact of difficult people extends beyond the immediate interaction. It can have a lasting effect on our overall mood and outlook on life. Prolonged exposure to difficult individuals may lead to chronic stress, whic can contribute to physical health issues such as high blood pressure, compromised immune function, and increased susceptibility to illnesses. Dealing with challenging individuals can emotionally drain us, making it harder for us to enjoy and be fulfilled in our endeavors.

Difficult people can also leave a mark on our relationships. Interactions with such individuals can create tension and conflict within our personal and professional circles. For example, dealing with a difficult colleague or supervisor in the workplace can lead to strained working relationships, reduced productivity, and a toxic work environment. In personal relationships, the impact of difficult people can lead to misunderstandings, arguments, and even the deterioration of once-close bonds.

In addition to affecting the quality of our relationships, difficult people can influence our behavior and self-perception. When confronted with aggression or manipulation, individuals may find themselves resorting to defensive or avoidance behaviors. They may second-guess their own actions and decisions, doubting their judgment or abilities. The constant need to adapt to the demands of difficult personalities can erode one's self-confidence and self-esteem over time.

Moreover, the impact of difficult people on our lives extends to our overall sense of well-being and life satisfaction. Constantly navigating challenging interactions can overshadow moments of joy and contentment. It may lead individuals to question the fairness of their circumstances and create a sense of helplessness or frustration. The emotional as well as psychological toll of dealing with difficult personalities can impact one's overall quality of life, making it difficult to enjoy the present moment fully.

It is worth noting that the impact of difficult people can vary in intensity and duration depending on the specific individuals involved and the coping strategies employed. Some individuals may possess a higher degree of resilience and emotional intelligence, allowing them to navigate difficult interactions with minimal long-term impact. Others may find coping more challenging and require external support or guidance to mitigate the effects.

In response to the impact of difficult people on our lives, it is essential to develop strategies for effective coping and resilience. One key aspect is recognizing the boundaries of our control. While we may not be able to change the difficult individuals themselves, we can control our responses and attitudes. Practicing self-awareness and emotional regulation can help mitigate the emotional toll of difficult interactions. Additionally, seeking support from trusted friends, family members, or mental health professionals can offer valuable guidance and a safe space to process emotions.

Setting clear boundaries is another crucial strategy for managing the impact of difficult people. Establishing boundaries helps protect one's mental and emotional well-being by defining acceptable behavior and interaction limits. Communicating these boundaries assertively and consistently is essential for maintaining healthy relationships and minimizing the negative effects of difficult personalities.

Furthermore, it is essential to remember that the impact of difficult people is not solely a burden; it can also be an opportunity for personal growth and resilience. Facing and navigating challenging interactions can lead to developing valuable life skills, such as conflict resolution, empathy, assertiveness, and emotional intelligence. These skills can be applied in dealing with difficult people and various other aspects of life.

In conclusion, the impact of difficult people on our lives is multifaceted and significant, affecting our emotional well-being, relationships, behavior, self-perception, and overall quality of life. While navigating difficult personalities can be challenging, it is essential to recognize the boundaries of our control, develop effective coping strategies, and seek support when needed. Moreover, viewing these challenges as opportunities for personal growth and skill development can empower individuals to manage the impact of difficult people and thrive in the face of adversity. Ultimately, our ability to navigate difficult personalities contributes to our resilience and emotional well-being, enhancing our capacity for more fulfilling and harmonious relationships.

CHAPTER II

Self-Reflection and Self-Awareness

The role of self-awareness in managing difficult interactions

Human interactions are a complex dance of emotions, perceptions, and communication. While many interactions are smooth and harmonious, we all encounter challenging situations involving difficult individuals at some point in our lives. In such encounters, the role of self-awareness becomes paramount. Self-awareness is the cornerstone of managing difficult interactions effectively, allowing individuals to navigate the intricate landscape of human relationships with greater understanding, empathy, and composure.

At its core, self-awareness is the ability to recognize and understand one's own thoughts, emotions, and behaviors. It involves taking a step back from a situation and introspectively examining our own reactions and motivations. In managing difficult interactions, self-awareness serves as a mirror that reflects our emotional responses and biases, enabling us to respond with greater clarity and control.

One of the fundamental aspects of self-awareness is recognizing our emotional triggers. Difficult individuals often have a knack for pushing our buttons and eliciting strong emotional reactions. These triggers can range from frustration and anger to anxiety and irritation. We can identify these triggers through self-awareness and understand why they affect us so deeply. For example, a difficult colleague's constant criticism may trigger feelings of inadequacy due to past experiences of rejection. Understanding this connection allows us to respond more rationally and empathetically, rather than reacting emotionally.

Self-awareness also involves acknowledging our own biases and preconceptions. We all have a lens through which we view the world, shaped by our upbringing, culture, and personal experiences. These biases can influence our perceptions of others and color our interactions. In managing difficult interactions, self-awareness prompts us to examine our biases and question whether they are influencing our judgments unfairly. For instance, if we hold preconceived notions about a particular personality type being difficult, we may inadvertently create a self-fulfilling prophecy in our interactions. Self-awareness allows us to challenge these biases and approach each interaction more openly and objectively.

Moreover, self-awareness empowers us to regulate our emotional responses. When faced with difficult individuals, it is natural to experience an array of emotions, from frustration to anger or even resentment. Without self-awareness, these emotions can take control of our reactions, leading to escalating conflicts and strained relationships. By recognizing our emotional responses as they arise, we can take a step back and choose how to respond consciously. This might entail taking a deep breath, counting to ten, or using positive self-talk to calm our emotions and maintain composure. In

addition to emotions, self-awareness extends to our communication style and patterns. Many difficult interactions are exacerbated by miscommunication or misunderstandings. Self-awareness prompts us to examine how we communicate and how our communication style may be contributing to the difficulty.

Are we being clear and assertive in expressing our needs and boundaries, or are we resorting to passive-aggressive or confrontational communication? By understanding our communication patterns, we can consciously improve our capacity to convey our thoughts and feelings effectively.

Furthermore, self-awareness encourages empathy. Empathy is known as the ability to understand and share the feelings of another person. Empathy is a potent tool for building bridges of understanding in managing difficult interactions. Self-awareness helps us put ourselves in the difficult individual's shoes, attempting to see the situation from their perspective. This is not the same as condoning or justifying their actions; rather, it is about attempting to comprehend any underlying fears or motivations that may be at play. Empathy fosters a more compassionate approach and can defuse tension in the interaction. Self-

awareness also plays a crucial role in setting and maintaining healthy boundaries. Difficult individuals may test boundaries or push limits; without self-awareness, we may struggle to assert our own needs and limits effectively. Self-awareness helps us recognize when our boundaries are being challenged and provides the clarity and strength to assert them firmly but respectfully. It enables us to communicate our boundaries in an assertive rather than aggressive way, helping to maintain the integrity of the interaction.

Moreover, self-awareness is a continuous process of growth and self-improvement. It involves an ongoing commitment to introspection and self-reflection. Through self-awareness, we can identify areas where we may need to develop new skills or change our perspectives. For example, if we tend to avoid difficult conversations, self-awareness can prompt us to work on our assertiveness and conflict resolution skills. If we struggle with patience, self-awareness can lead us to explore mindfulness techniques or stress management strategies.

In conclusion, the role of self-awareness in managing difficult interactions is indispensable. It serves as a mirror that reflects our emotional triggers, biases, communication patterns, and behaviors, enabling us to respond to difficult individuals with greater empathy, composure, and effectiveness. Self-awareness empowers us to recognize and regulate our emotional responses, challenge our biases, and communicate more effectively. It encourages empathy and the ability to see situations from multiple perspectives, fostering understanding and defusing tension. Ultimately, self-awareness is a powerful tool for personal growth and resilience in the face of challenging interactions, enriching our relationships and enhancing our capacity to navigate the intricate landscape of human connections.

Self-assessment exercises

Self-awareness is the cornerstone of personal development and successful interpersonal relationships. It entails a deep understanding of one's own thoughts, emotions, strengths, weaknesses, and motivations. While self-awareness can be naturally developed through life experiences, self-assessment exercises offer structured and intentional approaches to accelerate this process. These exercises serve as valuable tools in navigating the path to self-discovery, enhancing emotional intelligence, and fostering personal growth.

One of the most fundamental self-assessment exercises involves introspection. It is the process of self-reflection and self-examination, often through journaling or meditation. Introspection encourages individuals to set aside time for quiet contemplation, allowing them to explore their inner thoughts and feelings. This exercise can be particularly valuable in identifying recurring patterns of behavior, emotional triggers, and areas of personal interest or passion. Introspection provides the space for individuals to connect with their inner selves and also gain insights into their values and aspirations.

Another powerful self-assessment tool is the personality assessment. These assessments, like the Myers-Briggs Type Indicator (MBTI) or the Big Five Personality Traits, provide individuals with insights into their personality characteristics and preferences. By understanding their personality type, individuals can gain clarity on their communication style, decision-making processes, and interpersonal dynamics. These assessments highlight strengths and areas for growth, helping individuals make more informed choices in both personal and professional settings.

Furthermore, emotional intelligence assessments offer a structured way to evaluate one's emotional awareness and regulation. These assessments typically measure components such as self-awareness, self-regulation, empathy, and social skills. By taking an emotional intelligence assessment, individuals can gain a clearer picture of their emotional strengths and areas in need of improvement. This insight can be invaluable in managing interpersonal relationships, as it allows individuals to recognize and to navigate their own emotions while understanding the emotions of others.

Self-assessment exercises also extend to goal setting and self-reflection on achievements. Setting both short-term and long-term objectives provides a sense of direction and purpose. Tracking progress toward these goals through regular self-assessment allows individuals to celebrate successes, learn from setbacks, and make necessary adjustments. The process of setting as well as achieving goals fosters motivation and a sense of accomplishment, contributing to personal growth and development.

Values clarification exercises help individuals identify and prioritize their core values and beliefs. By examining what truly matters to them, individuals can align their actions and their decisions with their values, leading to a more fulfilling and authentic life. Values clarification exercises often involve making lists or answering thought-provoking questions that prompt individuals to consider what brings meaning as well as purpose to their lives.

Self-assessment exercises can also delve into specific areas of personal development, such as communication skills. For example, individuals can engage in exercises that assess their active listening abilities, assertiveness, or conflict resolution skills. These exercises often involve scenarios or role-play, allowing individuals to practice as well as refine their communication skills in a secure and controlled environment. As a result, they can become more effective communicators in their personal and professional relationships.

Furthermore, feedback-seeking exercises encourage individuals to seek input and constructive criticism from others actively. Getting feedback, whether from friends, mentors, or coworkers, provides an outside viewpoint that can highlight blind spots or potential improvement areas. By being open to feedback and actively seeking it, individuals can accelerate their personal growth and make informed adjustments to their behavior and actions.

Self-assessment exercises are not limited to individuals alone; they can also be valuable tools in improving teamwork and collaboration. Team-building exercises, such as the Belbin Team Role Self-Perception Inventory, allow team members to assess their individual roles and contributions within a group. This awareness can enhance team dynamics by helping individuals understand how their strengths can complement the strengths of others, leading to more effective collaboration and problem-solving.

Additionally, values-based decision-making exercises guide individuals in making choices that align with their core values. These exercises often present hypothetical scenarios or dilemmas, prompting individuals to consider how their values influence their decision-making process. Making decisions based on values ensures that people act ethically and with integrity by helping them make decisions that align with their inner values.

In conclusion, self-assessment exercises are powerful tools in the journey of self-discovery and personal growth. They offer structured and intentional approaches to developing self-awareness, emotional intelligence, and specific skills such as communication and values-based decision-making. By means of self-examination, personality evaluations, emotional intelligence assessments, goal setting, values clarification, and feedback-seeking activities, people can acquire significant understanding of their inner selves and make well-informed decisions that promote both interpersonal and personal growth. Through increased self-awareness, authenticity, and resilience, these exercises enable people to successfully navigate life's complexities, which ultimately improves their general well-being.

Recognizing your own triggers and biases

Human interactions are a dynamic interplay of emotions, experiences, and perspectives. In our interactions with others, we bring our own unique set of triggers and biases, which can significantly influence our reactions and judgments. Recognizing these triggers and biases is a critical step toward self-awareness and empathy. It allows us to navigate the complexities of human relationships with greater understanding, compassion, and open-mindedness.

Triggers, in the context of emotional responses, are specific situations or stimuli that activate intense emotional reactions. These reactions can be positive, such as joy or excitement, but they can also be negative, leading to emotions like anger, frustration, or anxiety. Triggers are often linked to past experiences, particularly those associated with trauma, significant life events, or long-standing patterns of behavior.

For instance, imagine someone who grew up in an environment where they experienced frequent criticism and judgment. In their adult life, they may find themselves triggered when receiving constructive feedback at work, interpreting it as a personal attack rather than a chance for improvement. In this scenario, the trigger is the criticism, and the emotional response is heightened due to past experiences.

On the other hand, biases refer to preconceived beliefs or judgments that affect our perceptions and interactions. These biases can be related to various aspects such as gender, race, age, religion, or even personal preferences. Biases often result from societal conditioning, cultural influences, and personal experiences, and they can manifest as stereotypes, prejudices, or discriminatory attitudes.

For instance, unconscious racial bias may lead someone to make assumptions or judgments about a person's abilities or character based on their race, even if they are not consciously aware of holding such beliefs. These biases can affect decisions, behavior, and interactions without the individual's explicit intent.

Recognizing one's own triggers and biases is an essential element of self-awareness. It involves the willingness to introspectively examine our emotional reactions and automatic judgments in various situations. By identifying our triggers, we gain insight into the specific circumstances that lead to strong emotional responses. This insight can be empowering, as it allows us to anticipate and manage our reactions more effectively.

For example, if someone recognizes that they have a trigger related to public speaking due to a past embarrassing experience, they can proactively work on managing their anxiety and discomfort when faced with such situations. This might involve seeking public speaking training or employing relaxation techniques to mitigate the emotional response triggered by the fear of embarrassment.

Similarly, recognizing biases within ourselves is essential to personal growth and empathy. It is not uncommon for individuals to be unaware of their biases or to resist acknowledging them due to discomfort or guilt. However, this recognition is a fundamental step in dismantling and overcoming biases.

Acknowledging biases can be a challenging process, but it is a necessary one. It involves examining our beliefs, attitudes, and stereotypes about others and considering how these biases influence our perceptions and behavior. For instance, someone may recognize a bias they hold about a particular nationality based on stereotypes they've encountered. By acknowledging this bias, they can consciously work to challenge and change these prejudiced beliefs.

Moreover, recognizing triggers and biases contributes to more empathetic and open-minded interactions with others. When we understand our own emotional triggers, we become better equipped to manage our reactions and avoid projecting our emotional responses onto others. This allows us to engage in more constructive and empathetic conversations, even in challenging situations.

In the workplace, for example, recognizing triggers related to authority figures can help individuals maintain composure and professionalism when receiving feedback or instructions from their superiors. This self-awareness enables them to address their emotional responses internally rather than reacting defensively or emotionally in the presence of their managers.

Similarly, acknowledging biases allows individuals to approach others more fairly and emotionally. When we recognize that our biases may be influencing our perceptions of someone, we can actively challenge those biases and strive to see the individual as they truly are, rather than through the lens of prejudice.

For instance, recognizing gender bias can prompt individuals to question assumptions about the capabilities or roles of people based on their gender. People can actively contribute to the creation of a more fair and inclusive society where people are evaluated on their character and abilities rather than on preconceived notions about gender by actively confronting these stereotypes.

In conclusion, recognizing your own triggers and biases is essential in the journey toward self-awareness and empathy. Triggers are the emotional responses that arise from specific situations, often tied to past experiences, while biases are preconceived beliefs that influence our perceptions and judgments. Identifying these triggers and biases empowers individuals to manage their emotional reactions more effectively and challenge prejudiced beliefs. It also enhances the quality of interactions with others, fostering greater understanding, compassion, and open-mindedness. By recognizing and addressing our own triggers and biases, we promote personal growth and contribute to creating a more inclusive and empathetic society where individuals are valued for their unique qualities as well as experiences.

CHAPTER III

Effective Communication

The foundation of peaceful coexistence

Peaceful coexistence is a fundamental aspiration of humanity, underpinning harmonious relationships within communities, nations, and across borders. At its core, peaceful coexistence is built upon a foundation of understanding, respect, and empathy. These pillars of human interaction enable individuals and societies to navigate the complexities of diverse perspectives, values, and beliefs while fostering a sense of unity and cooperation.

Understanding is the first cornerstone of peaceful coexistence. It involves the willingness and ability to comprehend the viewpoints, backgrounds, and experiences of others. Understanding goes beyond mere awareness; it requires active engagement and a commitment to gaining insights into the motivations and emotions that drive human behavior.

In peaceful coexistence, understanding encompasses an openness to diverse perspectives and an eagerness to learn from others. It means transcending the boundaries of one's own cultural, social, or personal norms to appreciate the rich tapestry of human diversity. It means realizing that each person has a distinct set of experiences that have shaped their opinions and behavior.

When individuals and communities prioritize understanding, they create an environment where differences can be embraced rather than feared. They recognize that dialogue and communication are essential tools for resolving conflicts and fostering cooperation. By actively seeking to understand others, individuals can bridge divides and build bridges of empathy and connection.

Respect is the second pillar of peaceful coexistence. It involves recognizing every individual's inherent worth and dignity, regardless of their background, beliefs, or characteristics. Respect is the foundation for human rights, equality, and justice.

Respect means valuing diversity and treating others with fairness, courtesy, and consideration in peaceful coexistence. It entails refraining from prejudice, discrimination, or harmful actions that undermine the well-being and rights of others. Respect also extends to the natural world and the environment, as the interconnectedness of all living beings is an essential aspect of a peaceful coexistence.

When respect is upheld as a core principle, it establishes just and equitable societies. It ensures that individuals can express their beliefs, participate in decision-making processes, and live free from discrimination and violence. Respect creates an atmosphere where individuals can thrive and contribute their distinct talents and perspectives to the collective good.

Empathy serves as the third pillar of peaceful coexistence. It is the capability to understand and share the feelings and experiences of others. Empathy requires individuals to step into another person's shoes, see the world through their eyes, and genuinely connect with their emotions.

Empathy fosters deep connections and a sense of shared humanity. It is the antidote to indifference, apathy, and cruelty. When individuals and societies prioritize empathy, they create a culture of care and compassion, where the suffering of others is not ignored but met with a genuine desire to help and alleviate pain.

In the context of peaceful coexistence, empathy is a potent tool for resolving conflicts and building bridges of understanding. It permits individuals to communicate their needs and concerns while also listening and responding to the needs and concerns of others. Empathy breaks down barriers and fosters a sense of interconnectedness, reminding us that, despite our differences, we share the universal experiences of joy, sorrow, love, and suffering.

Peaceful coexistence is not a passive state but an active commitment to upholding these three pillars: understanding, respect, and empathy. It requires individuals and societies to continuously reflect on their actions, values, and attitudes to create an environment where these principles can thrive.

However, the pursuit of peaceful coexistence is not without its challenges. It often involves confronting prejudice, discrimination, and injustice. People must be aware of their own biases and make an effort to overcome them. It demands patience, persistence, and the courage to stand up against hatred and intolerance.

Moreover, peaceful coexistence is not limited to the realm of individuals and communities. It extends to the global stage, where nations must work together to address issues such as conflict, inequality, climate change, and the protection of human rights. International diplomacy and cooperation are essential tools for promoting peace and harmony among nations.

In recent years, the world has witnessed remarkable progress and significant challenges in pursuing peaceful coexistence. While advancements in technology have connected people across the globe and facilitated dialogue and understanding, they have also given rise to new forms of conflict and polarization. Issues like racial inequality, social justice, and environmental sustainability have gained prominence, prompting urgent calls for change and reform.

In this context, the foundation of peaceful coexistence becomes even more critical. Understanding, respect, and empathy are the guiding principles that can help individuals and societies navigate these complex and turbulent times. They provide a roadmap for addressing conflicts and divisions while promoting unity and cooperation.

In conclusion, the foundation of peaceful coexistence is built upon the pillars of understanding, respect, and empathy. These principles guide individuals and societies in embracing diversity, upholding human rights, and fostering connections that transcend boundaries and differences. Peaceful coexistence is not a passive state but an active commitment to creating a world where all individuals can live with equality, dignity, and compassion. It is a journey that requires continuous reflection, growth, and the unwavering dedication to building a more just and harmonious world for present and future generations.

Active listening skills

Successful interpersonal and professional relationships are built on effective communication. At the heart of meaningful communication lies the skill of active listening. Active listening goes beyond merely hearing words; it involves a deliberate and empathetic effort to understand the speaker's message, emotions, and perspectives. This skill is instrumental in building rapport, resolving conflicts, and fostering deeper connections with others. In this section, we will explore the concept of active listening, its key components, and its far-reaching impact on various aspects of life.

Active listening is a communication skill that emphasizes not only hearing but also comprehending and responding to what the speaker is saying. It involves giving one's full attention to the speaker, both verbally and non-verbally, to convey genuine interest and understanding. Active listening encompasses various elements, each contributing to its effectiveness.

One of the primary components of active listening is attentive silence. This means giving the speaker the space and time to express themselves without interruptions or premature responses. Attentive silence allows the speaker to feel heard and respected, encouraging them to share their thoughts and feelings more openly. It also provides the listener with the opportunity to absorb the information being conveyed fully.

Verbal acknowledgments are another essential aspect of active listening. These include verbal cues such as nodding, affirmations like "I see," "I understand," and reflective statements like "So what you're saying is..." Verbal acknowledgments serve to validate the speaker's words and emotions, demonstrating empathy and a willingness to engage in the conversation. They signal to the speaker that their message is being received and acknowledged.

Additionally, paraphrasing and summarizing are crucial active listening techniques. Paraphrasing involves restating the speaker's message in one's own words to confirm understanding, while summarizing condenses the main points of the conversation. These techniques demonstrate active engagement and help clarify any potential misunderstandings and make sure that both parties are on the same page.

Asking open-ended questions is another key strategy in active listening. These questions invite the speaker to expand on their thoughts and provide more information. Open-ended questions encourage deeper reflection and allow for a richer and more comprehensive exchange of ideas. They demonstrate genuine interest in the speaker's perspective and encourage them to share more openly.

Non-verbal cues play a significant role in active listening. Maintaining eye contact, adopting an open and welcoming body posture, and using facial expressions that convey empathy all contribute to effective communication. Non-verbal cues signal to the speaker that their message is being received with care and attention. They help create an atmosphere of trust and openness, which is essential for productive conversations.

The impact of active listening extends to various aspects of life. In personal relationships, active listening fosters intimacy and connection. When individuals feel truly heard and understood by their partners, it strengthens their emotional bond. Active listening allows couples to constructively navigate conflicts and resolve disagreements with empathy and respect. It also promotes a sense of emotional safety, encouraging open and honest communication.

In friendships, active listening deepens trust and nurtures a supportive environment. Friends who actively listen to each other are more likely to provide comfort and understanding during challenging times. They can offer valuable insights and perspectives, enhancing the quality of their friendships. Active listening is also a way to celebrate each other's successes and joys, strengthening the positive aspects of the friendship.

In the workplace, active listening is an invaluable skill for effective teamwork and leadership. Team members who actively listen to each other are better equipped to collaborate and solve problems. They can understand each other's ideas and concerns, leading to more innovative and well-rounded solutions. In leadership roles, active listening fosters trust and employee engagement. Leaders who listen to their team members' feedback and ideas demonstrate respect and a commitment to their growth and well-being.

Active listening is a cornerstone of building strong client relationships in customer service and sales. Customers who feel heard as well as understood are more likely to trust and return to a business. Sales professionals who actively listen to their clients' needs can provide tailored solutions, enhancing customer satisfaction and loyalty. Active listening in customer service also helps resolve conflicts and complaints more effectively, leading to better outcomes for both parties.

In conflict resolution, active listening is pivotal in de-escalating tense situations and finding mutually agreeable solutions. When individuals in conflict feel heard and acknowledged, it reduces defensiveness and opens the door to productive dialogue. Active listening allows conflicting parties to express their grievances and perspectives, which is essential for reaching a resolution that satisfies all parties involved.

Moreover, active listening is a valuable skill in education and mentoring. Teachers who actively listen to their students create a supportive learning environment. Students who feel heard are more likely to engage in the learning process and express their questions and concerns. Mentors who actively listen to their mentees can provide guidance and support that is tailored to their needs and aspirations, facilitating personal and professional growth.

In healthcare, active listening is an essential component of patient-centered care. Patients' symptoms, concerns, and preferences can be better understood by healthcare professionals who actively listen to their patients. As a result, diagnosis and treatment strategies become more precise. Moreover, active listening in healthcare fosters trust and comfort, which is crucial for patients during their healthcare journey.

In conclusion, active listening is a powerful and transformative communication skill. It involves giving one's full attention to the speaker, using verbal and non- verbal cues to convey understanding, and employing various techniques such as paraphrasing and asking open-ended questions. Active listening is beneficial for personal relationships and various professional contexts, including the workplace, customer service, conflict resolution, education, mentoring, and healthcare. Its impact extends to enhancing connection, trust, empathy, and the quality of communication, ultimately leading to more meaningful and productive interactions in all areas of life.

Non-verbal communication cues

Communication is a multifaceted process that goes beyond words. While spoken and written language are undoubtedly essential, much of what we convey and understand in our interactions with others happens through non-verbal communication cues. These cues include a broad variety of signals, such as gestures, tone of voice, body language, and facial expressions. Non- verbal communication is a rich and intricate form of expression that significantly conveys emotions, intentions, and social dynamics. This section will explore the fascinating world of non-verbal communication cues, their importance, and their impact on our daily lives.

Facial Expressions are one of the most recognizable and powerful forms of non-verbal communication. Our faces can convey many emotions, from joy and surprise to anger and sadness. Microexpressions, fleeting facial expressions that last just a fraction of a second, can reveal genuine feelings that individuals may attempt to conceal consciously. The furrowing of brows, the curling of lips, and the widening of eyes are all indicators of the emotional landscape beneath the surface.

Beyond emotions, facial expressions can also communicate social cues. A warm smile can signify friendliness and approachability, while a furrowed brow may indicate concern or confusion. The eyes, often called the "windows to the soul," can convey trust, sincerity, or deception. Understanding facial expressions is crucial for interpreting the emotional state and intentions of others accurately.

Body Language encompasses a wide array of non-verbal cues conveyed through posture, gestures, and movements. Posture can communicate confidence, attentiveness, or relaxation. For example, standing tall with shoulders back typically suggests confidence, while slouching can signify indifference or fatigue. Gestures, such as nodding, waving, or pointing, complement verbal communication and can convey agreement, greeting, or direction.

Furthermore, body movements are instrumental in conveying emotions and intentions. For instance, how someone walks can reveal their mood – a brisk, purposeful stride may indicate determination, while slow, shuffling steps can signal sadness or exhaustion. Additionally, physical proximity and personal space, known as proxemics, play a role in non-verbal communication. The distance individuals maintain between each other can communicate intimacy or boundaries, with different cultures and contexts influencing what is considered appropriate.

Tone of Voice is another crucial non-verbal cue that significantly impacts communication. The way words are spoken, including pitch, volume, speed, and intonation, can convey a wealth of information beyond the literal meaning of the words. For example, a soft-spoken, melodic tone may signal calmness or affection, while a sharp, loud tone can indicate anger or frustration.

In addition to conveying emotions, tone of voice can clarify the speaker's intentions. A rising intonation at the end of a sentence, known as uptalk, may suggest a question or uncertainty, while a descending intonation conveys a statement or confidence. Variations in tone can also be used to emphasize certain words or phrases, highlighting their significance in the message.

Eye Contact is a non-verbal cue that is critical in interpersonal communication. The eyes can convey interest, attentiveness, or engagement. Direct and prolonged eye contact can signal confidence and sincerity, while avoiding eye contact may be interpreted as discomfort, shyness, or dishonesty.

However, the significance of eye contact varies across cultures and contexts. Extended eye contact can be interpreted as invasive or confrontational depending on the culture in which it occurs. In some, it is seen as a sign of respect and attentiveness. Therefore, understanding cultural norms and context is essential when interpreting the meaning of eye contact.

Touch is a powerful non-verbal cue that conveys a wide range of emotions and intentions. Physical contact, such as a handshake, hug, or pat on the back, can communicate warmth, affection, or congratulations. The significance of touch varies across cultures and relationships, with different norms dictating the appropriateness of physical contact.

A firm handshake is frequently seen as a sign of confidence and professionalism in professional settings. In personal relationships, a gentle touch on the arm can convey empathy and support. However, it is crucial to respect personal boundaries and consent when using touch as a form of non-verbal communication.

Proxemics, as mentioned earlier, refers to the use of personal space in non-verbal communication. Different cultures and individuals have varying comfort zones when it comes to physical proximity. Understanding these boundaries is essential for respecting personal space and ensuring comfortable interactions.

In crowded environments, such as public transportation, individuals may adapt to closer proximity due to limited space. In contrast, maintaining an appropriate distance is crucial to ensure comfort and respect in more intimate settings, such as a one-on-one conversation.

Paralanguage encompasses non-verbal cues related to speech, including vocal pitch, rate of speech, and vocal quality. These cues can convey emotions and intentions beyond the words spoken. For example, a quivering voice may indicate nervousness or fear, while a slow, deliberate pace may suggest seriousness or emphasis.
Vocal pitch and intonation can also convey nuances in meaning. A statement can become a question at the end of a sentence if the pitch rises, whereas a monotone voice can convey boredom or indifference. Paralanguage is a valuable aspect of non-verbal communication that adds depth and subtlety to verbal messages.
Artifacts, such as clothing, accessories, and personal items, can also convey non-verbal cues about an individual's identity, values, and social status. Clothing choices, for instance, can communicate cultural affiliations, professional roles, or personal preferences. Accessories, such as jewelry or tattoos, may hold personal significance and convey aspects of one's identity.

In conclusion, non-verbal communication cues are a rich and intricate form of expression that significantly influence our interactions with others. The unspoken language of human interaction is influenced by proxemics, paralanguage, body language, eye contact, touch, tone of voice, and artifacts. These cues convey emotions, intentions, social dynamics, and cultural nuances, adding depth and complexity to our communication. Understanding and interpreting non-verbal cues is essential for effective communication, empathy, and building meaningful connections with others.

Building empathy

Empathy is a potent and transformational attribute that enables people to comprehend and relate to the thoughts, feelings, and viewpoints of others. It is the capacity to put oneself in another person's position, view the world from their perspective, and establish a more profound emotional connection. Building empathy is essential for fostering meaningful relationships, resolving conflicts, and promoting understanding in our increasingly diverse and interconnected world. In this section, we will explore the concept of empathy, its significance, and strategies for cultivating this vital skill.

Empathy, often explained as the "ability to walk in someone else's shoes," involves both cognitive and emotional elements. Cognitive empathy is the capacity to comprehend another person's perspective, thoughts, and feelings. On the other hand, emotional empathy involves feeling the emotions that another person is experiencing. Together, these dimensions of empathy enable individuals to connect with others on a profound level.

Empathy is the foundation of compassion and altruism, driving individuals to take action to alleviate the suffering of others. When we empathize with someone in distress, it motivates us to offer support, comfort, and assistance. Compassionate acts are often driven by the genuine desire to mitigate the pain and suffering of others, reflecting the interconnectedness of humanity.

Intimacy and trust are developed through empathy in interpersonal relationships. People's emotional bonds are strengthened when they feel their partners understand and validate them. Empathetic listening allows couples to navigate conflicts more constructively, encouraging open communication and acknowledging each other's perspectives. It also fosters a sense of emotional safety, enabling individuals to share their vulnerabilities and fears.

In parent-child relationships, empathy is essential for effective parenting. Parents who empathize with their children can better understand their needs, fears, and joys. This understanding allows parents to provide emotional support, guidance, and validation, which are critical for a child's emotional and social development. Empathetic parenting nurtures a secure attachment between parents and children, fostering resilience and emotional well-being.

In friendships, empathy is the glue that binds individuals together. Friends who empathize with each other provide comfort, support, and a listening ear during challenging times. They celebrate each other's successes and joys genuinely. Empathetic friends offer a sense of belonging and validation, which is vital for mental and emotional health.

In the workplace, empathy is a valuable skill for effective teamwork and leadership. Team members who empathize with each other are better equipped to collaborate and solve problems. They can understand each other's perspectives and concerns, leading to more innovative and well-rounded solutions. In leadership roles, empathy fosters trust and employee engagement. Leaders who empathize with their team members demonstrate respect and a commitment to their growth and well-being.

Empathy is a fundamental component of effective communication. When we empathize with others, it encourages active listening and a willingness to understand their point of view. Empathetic communication is characterized by non-judgmental listening, validation of emotions, and acknowledgment of the speaker's perspective. This form of communication promotes understanding and minimizes miscommunication and conflicts.

Conflict resolution benefits significantly from empathy. When individuals in conflict feel heard and understood, it reduces defensiveness and opens the door to productive dialogue. Empathetic listening allows conflicting parties to express their grievances and perspectives, which is essential for reaching a resolution that satisfies all parties involved. Mediators and negotiators often rely on empathy to facilitate successful conflict resolution. Empathy is instrumental in social justice and promoting equality. Empathizing with individuals who have experienced discrimination or injustice allows us to understand their struggles and advocate for change. Empathy motivates individuals and communities to stand up against inequality and work toward a fairer and more inclusive society.

Cultural empathy is a specific form of empathy that involves understanding and appreciating cultural differences. In an increasingly globalized world, cultural empathy is essential for building bridges across cultures and promoting cultural diversity and inclusion. It allows individuals to navigate diverse cultural contexts with respect and sensitivity.

Self-empathy, or self-compassion, is the capacity to extend empathy to oneself. It involves treating oneself with the same kindness and understanding that one would offer to others. Self-empathy acknowledges one's own struggles, flaws, and imperfections without self-criticism or judgment. Cultivating self-empathy is vital for mental and emotional well-being, as it promotes self-acceptance and resilience.

Building empathy is not a fixed trait but a skill that can be cultivated and developed over time. Here are some strategies for cultivating empathy:

Active Listening: Pay attention to what others are saying without interrupting or passing judgment. Give your full attention to the speaker and validate their feelings and perspectives.

Practice Perspective-Taking: Try to see the world from someone else's point of view. Imagine what it feels like to be in their situation and consider their emotions and thoughts.

Engage in Open-Minded Conversations: Seek out conversations and interactions with people from varied backgrounds and perspectives. Engaging with different viewpoints can broaden your understanding and empathy.

Read Literature and Stories: Literature, fiction, and biographies offer insights into the lives and the experiences of others. Reading stories from various cultures and backgrounds can enhance empathy.

Volunteer and Participate in Community Service: Participating in community service and volunteer work provides opportunities to connect with people facing various challenges. It allows you to witness and empathize with their experiences.

Practice Mindfulness: Mindfulness meditation can increase self-awareness and emotional regulation, which are essential components of empathy.

Reflect on Your Own Experiences: Consider your own experiences of pain, joy, and struggle. Reflecting on your emotions and challenges can help you relate to others' experiences more empathetically.

In conclusion, empathy is a profound and transformative quality that enables individuals to connect with others on a deep emotional level. It is instrumental in building meaningful relationships, resolving conflicts, and fostering understanding in personal, professional, and societal contexts. Empathy is a skill that can be developed through active listening, perspective-taking, open- mindedness, and engagement with diverse perspectives. It is a powerful force for promoting compassion, social justice, and positive human connections, ultimately contributing to a more empathetic and interconnected world.

CHAPTER IV

Conflict Resolution Strategies

Approaches to resolving conflicts peacefully

Conflict is an inherent part of human interaction, and throughout history, various approaches have been employed to resolve conflicts peacefully. These approaches aim to avoid violence, promote understanding, and achieve mutually beneficial outcomes. This section will explore several key approaches to resolving conflicts peacefully, ranging from negotiation and mediation to diplomacy and nonviolent resistance.

One of the most commonly used methods for resolving conflicts peacefully is negotiation. Negotiation involves parties coming together to discuss their differences and reach a mutually acceptable agreement. It is a constructive approach that allows conflicting parties to communicate openly, express their concerns, and seek common ground. Successful negotiation often requires compromise, where each party gives up something to gain something in return. Negotiation can be applied in various settings, from international diplomacy to business contracts and personal relationships. It provides an opportunity for conflicting parties to find win-win solutions and maintain relationships.

Mediation is another valuable approach to peaceful conflict resolution. Mediation entails the intervention of a neutral third party who allows for communication between the conflicting parties. The mediator assists the parties explore their interests, clarify their needs, and generate potential solutions. In contrast to an arbitrator or judge, a mediator does not impose a decision but encourages the parties to find their own resolution. Mediation is particularly useful in family disputes, workplace conflicts, and community disagreements. It fosters a sense of ownership over the resolution and often leads to more enduring agreements.

Diplomacy is crucial in resolving conflicts at the international level. Diplomatic efforts involve negotiations, communication, and engagement between countries or international organizations. Diplomats work to build relationships, find common ground, and prevent conflicts from escalating into wars. Multilateral diplomacy, where multiple parties are involved in negotiations, is often employed to address complex global issues including climate change and nuclear disarmament. Diplomacy requires patience, persistence, and skilled diplomats who can navigate the complexities of international relations.

Nonviolent resistance is a powerful approach to resolving conflicts without resorting to violence. This strategy, popularized by figures like Mahatma Gandhi and Martin Luther King Jr., involves using nonviolent methods such as protests, civil disobedience, and boycotts to challenge oppressive systems and demand change. Nonviolent resistance seeks to expose injustice, mobilize public support, and create moral pressure on the oppressor to change their behavior. It has been instrumental in achieving civil rights, overthrowing oppressive regimes, and advancing social justice causes. Nonviolent resistance demonstrates the power of peaceful collective action.

Restorative justice is an approach that concentrates on repairing harm caused by conflicts and restoring relationships. Instead of punitive measures, restorative justice involves bringing together the victim, offender, and the community to discuss the impact of the conflict and find ways to make amends. This approach is often used in criminal justice systems as an alternative to incarceration, aiming to rehabilitate offenders and reintegrate them into society. Restorative justice emphasizes accountability, empathy, and healing, making it a valuable tool in resolving conflicts while addressing the underlying causes.

Another approach to peaceful conflict resolution is arbitration. In arbitration, a disagreement is submitted to an impartial arbiter who renders a legally-binding judgment after considering the proof and points raised by each party. In arbitration, the arbitrator is the one who make the final decision; in mediation, the parties decide how the matter will be resolved. It is frequently employed in labor disputes, business disputes, and contract disputes. Arbitration offers a quicker and more private resolution compared to court litigation, making it an attractive option for many.

In conclusion, conflicts are an inevitable part of human existence, but they can be resolved peacefully through various approaches. Negotiation and mediation encourage open communication and compromise, while diplomacy seeks to prevent international conflicts through dialogue and engagement. Nonviolent resistance has proven effective in challenging oppressive systems, and restorative justice focuses on healing and repairing relationships. Arbitration offers a formalized process for resolving disputes in a binding manner. These approaches demonstrate that violence is not the only option, and through dialogue, understanding, and cooperation, conflicts can be resolved peacefully, leading to better outcomes for all parties involved.

Negotiation techniques

Negotiation is a fundamental component of human interaction, whether it occurs in our personal relationships, business transactions, or international diplomacy. The ability to negotiate efficiently can lead to mutually beneficial outcomes and strengthen relationships. In this section, we will explore various negotiation techniques that individuals and organizations employ to achieve successful outcomes.

Effective communication is a crucial negotiating tactic. Successful negotiations start with open and transparent communication. Parties involved in a negotiation must express their needs, interests, and concerns transparently. Active listening is equally important; it involves attentively hearing and understanding the other party's perspective. Through active listening, negotiators can identify common ground and areas of potential compromise. Effective communication also includes asking clarifying questions and paraphrasing to ensure that both sides are on the same page.

Another crucial negotiation technique is preparation. Successful negotiators invest time in researching and collecting information about the subject matter, the other party, and potential alternatives. This preparation helps negotiators anticipate arguments, counterarguments, and possible objections. By understanding the context and the interests of all parties involved, negotiators can enter the negotiation room with a clear strategy and a higher likelihood of achieving their objectives.

The concept of BATNA, also known as Best Alternative to a Negotiated Agreement, is a critical negotiation technique. BATNA represents the alternative course of action a negotiator can pursue if the current negotiation does not yield a satisfactory result. Understanding one's BATNA is essential because it provides a baseline for assessing the desirability of the negotiated agreement. A strong BATNA empowers negotiators, as it gives them the option to walk away from a deal that does not meet their needs. On the other hand, a weak BATNA may force negotiators into accepting unfavorable terms.

Building rapport as well as establishing a positive relationship with the other party is a valuable negotiation technique. People are more likely to make concessions and collaborate when they trust and feel comfortable with their counterparts. Building rapport involves finding common ground, being respectful, and showing empathy. It is essential to develop an atmosphere of mutual respect and cooperation, as it can lead to more productive negotiations and better long-term relationships.

A widely used negotiation technique is the art of concessions. Negotiators often need to give up something to gain something in return. Concessions can take various forms, such as compromising on price, adjusting timelines, or modifying terms and conditions. Skilled negotiators strategically time their concessions to show flexibility and goodwill while still protecting their core interests. Concessions can help build trust and move the negotiation toward a mutually beneficial agreement.

Negotiation techniques also encompass the use of persuasion and influence. Persuasion involves presenting compelling arguments and evidence to convince the other party of the merits of one's position. Influence, on the other hand, focuses on subtly shaping the other party's perception and decision-making process. Techniques such as reciprocity, consistency, and social proof can be leveraged to influence the other party's behavior and decisions. Successful negotiators use persuasion and influence ethically and effectively to advance their objectives.

Managing emotions is a critical negotiation technique. Emotions can run high during negotiations, and they can either facilitate or hinder the process. Skilled negotiators remain calm and composed, even in the face of adversity. They acknowledge and address their own emotions and those of the other party. Emotional intelligence, which involves recognizing and regulating emotions, is an asset in negotiation. It enables negotiators to navigate tense situations and maintain a constructive atmosphere.

Creativity and problem-solving skills are essential negotiation techniques, particularly in complex negotiations. Sometimes, the apparent solution is not readily apparent, and negotiators must find innovative ways to address both parties' interests. Brainstorming, exploring alternative options, and seeking mutually beneficial trade-offs are strategies that can lead to creative solutions. The ability to think outside the box can result in win-win outcomes that may not have been initially evident.

Negotiation techniques also include the practice of anchoring and framing. Anchoring involves presenting the first offer in a negotiation, which can serve as a reference point for subsequent discussions. Skilled negotiators use anchoring strategically to set a favorable starting point or frame the negotiation in their favor. Framing, on the other hand, involves shaping the context and perception of the negotiation. By framing the issues and solutions in a positive light, negotiators can influence the other party's perspective and preferences.

In conclusion, negotiation is a dynamic and multifaceted process that requires a range of techniques for success. Effective communication, preparation, understanding BATNA, building rapport, making concessions, persuasion, emotional management, creativity, and strategic anchoring and framing are all essential elements of successful negotiation. These techniques can be applied in various contexts, from resolving personal conflicts to achieving business deals and international agreements. By mastering these techniques, individuals and organizations can navigate negotiations with confidence and achieve outcomes that meet their objectives while maintaining positive relationships with their counterparts.

De-escalation tactics

De-escalation tactics are critical tools for defusing tense situations and preventing conflicts from escalating into violence. These techniques are employed in various contexts, from law enforcement and security to interpersonal conflicts and customer service. De-escalation tactics focus on communication, empathy, and problem-solving to reduce tension and promote a peaceful resolution. In this section, we will explore the principles and strategies of de-escalation, emphasizing their importance in today's complex and interconnected world.

The foundation of effective de-escalation tactics lies in clear and respectful communication. De-escalators aim to establish rapport and open channels of dialogue with individuals who may be agitated, upset, or confrontational. It is crucial to use active listening skills, which involve attentively hearing and understanding the other person's perspective. This helps build trust and also demonstrates that their concerns are being heard and valued. By showing respect and empathy, de-escalators create an environment in which individuals will likely cooperate and express themselves without resorting to aggression.

Another essential aspect of de-escalation is maintaining a calm and composed demeanor. De-escalators should regulate their own emotions and reactions, even when faced with hostility or provocation. Remaining calm sends a powerful signal to the other party that the situation can be managed without resorting to violence. It also allows de-escalators to think clearly and make informed decisions. This self-control is particularly vital for professionals in roles that involve conflict management, such as law enforcement officers and security personnel.

Empathy is a cornerstone of effective de-escalation tactics. Understanding the emotions and perspectives of the individuals involved in a conflict can go a long way in diffusing tensions. Empathetic de-escalators acknowledge the feelings and experiences of others without judgment. They seek to connect on a human level, recognizing that emotions often underlie aggressive behavior. By expressing empathy and validating the other person's emotions, de-escalators can help individuals feel heard and understood, reducing their need to escalate the conflict.

De-escalation tactics often involve active problem-solving. De-escalators collaborate with the parties concerned to identify the root causes of the conflict and consider potential solutions. This strategy transfers the emphasis from conflict to resolution. Problem-solving may include offering alternatives, seeking compromises, or finding common ground. By involving the conflicting parties in finding solutions, de-escalators empower them to take ownership of the process and work toward a mutually agreeable outcome.

Respect for personal boundaries is a fundamental principle of de-escalation tactics. Individuals in distress may have different comfort zones and triggers, and it is essential to respect their personal space and limits. In situations involving law enforcement, for instance, respecting personal boundaries can prevent confrontations from turning violent. De-escalators should use non-threatening body language and tone of voice, avoiding gestures or language that may be perceived as aggressive or intimidating.

Time and patience are often key elements of successful de-escalation. Rushing the process can lead to heightened tension and resistance. De-escalators should be prepared to invest the necessary time to build rapport, understand the underlying issues, and allow emotions to settle. Sometimes, simply providing individuals with space and time to cool off can be an effective de-escalation tactic.

De-escalation tactics must be adaptable to the specific context and individuals involved. What works in one situation may not work in another. De-escalators should be trained to assess the dynamics of each conflict and adjust their approach accordingly. Flexibility is crucial, as it allows de-escalators to respond effectively to changing circumstances and the unique needs of each situation.

Training and education are crucial components of implementing successful de-escalation tactics. Professionals in roles that involve conflict management should receive comprehensive training in de-escalation techniques. This training should cover communication skills, active listening, empathy-building, and scenario-based exercises. Continuous education and skill development are essential to ensure that individuals remain proficient in de-escalation tactics and can adapt to evolving situations and challenges.

In some cases, de-escalation tactics may not be successful, and the situation may continue to escalate. In such instances, de-escalators should have contingency plans in place to guarantee the safety of all parties involved. These plans may involve calling for additional assistance, such as law enforcement or medical personnel, to address the situation. Safety should always be the top priority, and de-escalators should be trained to recognize when a situation requires a different level of intervention.

The importance of de-escalation tactics extends beyond individual interactions to broader societal contexts. In recent years, there has been a growing recognition of the need for de-escalation in law enforcement and security operations. The use of force should always be a last resort, and de-escalation tactics can help reduce instances of unnecessary violence and fatalities.

Furthermore, de-escalation tactics have relevance in international diplomacy and conflict resolution. Diplomats and negotiators often employ de-escalation strategies when dealing with contentious issues between countries. The principles of clear communication, empathy, and problem-solving can help prevent conflicts from escalating into armed disputes and promote peaceful resolutions.

In conclusion, de-escalation tactics are valuable tools for diffusing tension and resolving conflicts peacefully. These tactics emphasize clear and respectful communication, empathy, problem-solving, and maintaining a calm demeanor. De-escalation is applicable in a wide range of contexts, from interpersonal conflicts to law enforcement, security, and international diplomacy. Training and education are essential to equip individuals with the skills and knowledge needed to effectively implement de-escalation tactics. By prioritizing de-escalation, we can contribute to a safer and more peaceful society, where conflicts are resolved through dialogue and understanding rather than violence.

Case studies of successful conflict resolution

Conflict is an inherent part of human interaction, and throughout history, individuals and groups have successfully resolved conflicts through various means. These case studies illustrate how conflict resolution techniques, such as negotiation, mediation, diplomacy, and nonviolent resistance, have been applied in different contexts to achieve peaceful outcomes and promote positive change.

One remarkable case study of successful conflict resolution is the negotiation and reconciliation process that took place in South Africa during the transition from apartheid to democracy. Under Nelson Mandela's direction, the African National Congress (or ANC) engaged in negotiations with the apartheid government to end racial segregation and establish a democratic and inclusive system. The negotiations, which took place between 1990 and 1994, were a testament to the power of negotiation and compromise in resolving deeply entrenched conflicts.

Key to the success of this negotiation was the commitment of both sides to finding a peaceful solution. Mandela and his counterparts recognized that a violent struggle would only result in further bloodshed and suffering. The negotiations focused on dismantling apartheid policies, establishing democratic elections, and ensuring equal rights for all South Africans. While challenging, the negotiation process ultimately led to the historic 1994 elections, which marked the end of apartheid and the beginning of a new era of reconciliation and nation-building in South Africa.

Another case study of successful conflict resolution is the Dayton Agreement, which ended the Bosnian War in 1995. The conflict in Bosnia-Herzegovina was a complex and devastating ethnic conflict that involved multiple parties with deep-rooted grievances. Diplomats from the United States, Europe, and Russia played a crucial part in brokering the agreement.

The Dayton Agreement, signed in Dayton, Ohio, established a framework for peace, territorial divisions, and power-sharing arrangements among the different ethnic groups in Bosnia. It also led to the creation of the Office of the High Representative, which oversaw the implementation of the agreement. While the peace process was far from perfect and faced numerous challenges, the Dayton Agreement succeeded in bringing an end to the violent conflict and providing a basis for a post-war Bosnia.

Mediation played a pivotal role in resolving the conflict between the government of Colombia as well as the Revolutionary Armed Forces of Colombia (or FARC). The Colombian conflict had persisted for more than five decades, resulting in countless casualties and widespread suffering. In 2012, negotiations facilitated by Cuba and Norway commenced in Havana, aiming to bring an end to the conflict.

The peace talks focused on issues such as rural development, political participation, and transitional justice. Mediators created a space for the Colombian government and FARC representatives to engage in direct dialogue and find common ground. After several years of negotiations and multiple ceasefires, the parties reached a historic peace agreement in 2016. While the agreement faced challenges during its implementation, it marked a significant step toward ending a protracted conflict that had plagued Colombia for generations.

An example of nonviolent resistance as a strategy for resolving conflict is the American civil rights movement. With the assistance of leaders like Martin Luther King Jr., the movement aimed to eradicate racial discrimination and segregation by using peaceful demonstrations, marches, and acts of civil disobedience. The 1963 March on Washington for Jobs and Freedom, during which Dr. King gave his well-known "I Have a Dream" speech, is among the movement's most iconic events.

The civil rights movement's nonviolent strategies attracted a lot of public support and brought attention to the injustices of segregation. Because of the movement's dedication to nonviolence and civil disobedience, important laws, such as the Voting Rights Act of 1965 and the Civil Rights Act of 1964, were eventually passed. A significant step toward racial equality and the abolition of segregation in the US was taken with the passage of these legal reforms.

In another case study of successful conflict resolution, we can examine the peace process that ended the Mozambican Civil War. The war, which lasted from 1977 to 1992, was characterized by intense violence and suffering. The peace negotiations, facilitated by the United Nations, brought together the Mozambican government and the rebel group known as RENAMO.

The negotiations led to the Rome General Peace Accords in 1992, which included provisions for a ceasefire, the disarmament of rebel forces, and the reintegration of former combatants into civilian life. The peace process also addressed key issues such as political representation, social reintegration, and economic development. While challenges remained in the post-war period, the successful negotiation and implementation of the peace agreement laid the foundation for stability and development in Mozambique.

These case studies of successful conflict resolution demonstrate that various approaches, including negotiation, mediation, diplomacy, and nonviolent resistance, can be effective in resolving even the most challenging and protracted conflicts. In each of these cases, individuals and groups recognized the futility of continued violence and sought alternative paths to peace and justice. These examples remind us that conflict resolution is not only possible but can lead to transformative change and reconciliation, offering hope for a more peaceful and just world.

CHAPTER V

Managing Emotions

Emotion regulation

Emotions are an integral part of the human experience. They shape our perceptions, influence our decisions, and drive our behavior. Emotions can be powerful motivators, guiding us toward desirable outcomes, but they can also be sources of distress when they become overwhelming or difficult to manage. Emotion regulation is the process by which individuals modulate, monitor, and manage their emotions to achieve desired emotional states and cope with emotional challenges. In this section, we will explore the concept of emotion regulation, its importance in mental well-being, and various strategies and techniques for effective emotion regulation.

Emotion regulation encompasses a wide range of processes aimed at influencing the intensity, duration, and expression of emotions. It involves both conscious and unconscious strategies that individuals use to adapt to changing emotional states and circumstances. Emotion regulation is not only about suppressing or denying emotions but rather it is about understanding and navigating them in a healthy and adaptive manner. The ability to control emotions effectively is essential for mental health and overall well-being.

One fundamental aspect of emotion regulation is emotional awareness. This involves recognizing and acknowledging one's emotions as they arise. Emotions can be fleeting and subtle, or they can be intense and overwhelming. Emotional awareness allows individuals to identify their emotional responses to different situations and stimuli. It involves naming the emotion, understanding its triggers, and being in touch with the physical sensations associated with it, such as changes in heart rate or muscle tension.

Closely related to emotional awareness is emotional acceptance. Acceptance involves allowing oneself to experience and feel emotions without judgment or criticism. It is the recognition that all emotions, even the negative ones, are valid and part of the human experience. Emotional acceptance does not mean condoning harmful actions or decisions driven by emotions but rather acknowledging the existence of those emotions as a starting point for regulation.

Once individuals are aware of their emotions and have accepted them, they can employ various strategies for effective emotion regulation. One common strategy is cognitive reappraisal. Reappraisal involves reframing or changing the way one thinks about a situation or event to influence the emotional response. For example, if faced with a challenging task, individuals can reframe it as a possibility for growth as well as learning rather than as a source of stress. This cognitive shift can result in a more positive emotional response.

Another widely used strategy is expressive suppression. Suppression involves consciously inhibiting the outward expression of emotions, particularly in social or professional settings. While suppression can be useful in certain situations, such as concealing anger during a professional meeting, it is not a recommended long-term strategy. Suppressing emotions can lead to emotional buildup, increased stress, and negative impacts on mental health.

A third strategy for emotion regulation is emotion-focused coping. This approach involves directing one's attention and efforts toward managing and processing the emotion itself. It may include engaging in activities that provide comfort or relaxation, seeking social support, or engaging in creative outlets like writing or art. Emotion-focused coping can be particularly helpful in dealing with intense emotions, grief, or trauma.

In contrast, problem-focused coping is a strategy that aims to address the underlying source of emotional distress. It involves taking concrete steps to change the situation or resolve the problem that is causing the emotional response. Problem-focused coping is effective when the emotion is related to a specific issue that can be addressed through action. For example, if financial stress is causing anxiety, individuals can create a budget and seek financial advice to alleviate the problem.

Social support is a crucial element of emotion regulation. Because we are social creatures, relationships with other people have a big impact on our emotional health. Speaking with loved ones, friends, or mental health specialists can offer a secure setting for expressing feelings, gaining perspective, and getting support. Emotional regulation deficiencies are frequently linked to feelings of loneliness and isolation, which can be lessened by sharing emotions with others.

The benefits of mindfulness and meditation techniques for controlling emotions are becoming more widely acknowledged. Being mindful is being aware of one's thoughts, feelings, as well as physical sensations in the present moment without passing judgment on them. By practicing mindfulness, individuals can become more attuned to their emotions and learn to observe them without reacting impulsively. This increased self-awareness and self-regulation can lead to greater emotional resilience.

Emotion regulation is not a one-size-fits-all process; it varies from person to person and situation to situation. What works for one individual may not work for another, and the effectiveness of emotion regulation strategies depends on various factors, including personality traits, cultural background, and the specific emotions involved. Some individuals may naturally excel at regulating their emotions, while others may need to consciously develop and refine their skills.

Emotion regulation is not only about managing negative emotions but also about enhancing positive emotions. Positive emotions, like joy, gratitude, and contentment, contribute to mental well-being and resilience. Strategies like savoring positive experiences, engaging in acts of kindness, and practicing gratitude can help individuals amplify their positive emotions and build emotional well-being over time.

In conclusion, emotion regulation is a multifaceted and essential aspect of human psychology and mental health. It involves processes of emotional awareness, acceptance, and the application of various strategies for managing emotions effectively. Emotion regulation is not about eliminating negative emotions but about developing skills to navigate them in a healthy and adaptive manner. By understanding and practicing emotion regulation, individuals can improve their mental well-being, enhance their interpersonal relationships, and lead more fulfilling lives. It is a lifelong journey of self-discovery and self-care that can lead to greater emotional resilience and happiness.

Coping mechanisms for dealing with difficult people

Difficult people are a common presence in our lives, whether they are colleagues, family members, friends, or strangers. These individuals can be challenging to interact with, often causing stress, frustration, and conflict. However, learning how to effectively cope with difficult people can significantly improve our interpersonal relationships, communication skills, and overall well-being. This section will explore coping mechanisms and strategies that can help individuals navigate interactions with difficult people in a constructive and emotionally healthy manner.

One essential coping mechanism for dealing with difficult people is active listening. Active listening entails giving the person your full attention, maintaining eye contact, and genuinely trying to understand their perspective. When we actively listen, we create a space for the difficult person to express themselves and feel heard. This can help defuse tension and open the door to more productive communication. It's important to resist the urge to interrupt or immediately respond with counterarguments. Instead, let the person finish speaking before you express your thoughts.

Empathy is another powerful tool for coping with difficult people. Empathy entails putting yourself in the other person's shoes and trying to comprehend their feelings and point of view. It's about recognizing that everyone has their own struggles, insecurities, and fears that may be driving their difficult behavior. You can express your concern for their feelings and willingness to consider things from their point of view by exhibiting empathy. This can lead to a more empathetic response from the difficult person and create a foundation for more constructive interactions.

Setting boundaries is a crucial coping mechanism when dealing with difficult people. Personal limits known as boundaries indicate what you will and won't put up with in a relationship or other interaction. When someone is consistently difficult or toxic, it's essential to establish and communicate clear boundaries to protect your well-being. This may involve limiting your contact with the person, asserting your need for respect and consideration, or even ending the relationship if necessary. Setting boundaries is an act of self-care that can prevent further harm and stress.

Remaining calm and composed is often easier said than done when dealing with difficult people, but it is a highly effective coping mechanism. Difficult individuals may try to provoke anger or emotional reactions, but responding with anger or frustration often escalates the situation. By staying calm and collected, you retain control over your emotions and can respond more thoughtfully and rationally. Deep breaths, mindfulness techniques, and self-regulation practices can help you maintain your composure in challenging interactions.

It's also essential to practice assertiveness when coping with difficult people. Assertiveness involves expressing your thoughts, needs, and feelings in a clear, respectful, and honest manner. It allows you to assert your boundaries and advocate for yourself without resorting to aggression or passive-aggressiveness. When you communicate assertively, you convey your perspective while also being open to a constructive dialogue. This can be particularly helpful in cases where the difficult person's behavior directly affects you or your well-being.

In some cases, it may be helpful to depersonalize the difficult person's behavior. Recognize that their actions and words may be more about their own issues, insecurities, or struggles than a direct attack on you. By depersonalizing the situation, you can detach yourself emotionally and view their behavior with a degree of objectivity. This can reduce the emotional impact of their actions and allow you to respond more calmly and empathetically.

Finding common ground is a valuable coping mechanism when dealing with difficult people. Even in challenging interactions, there are often areas of shared interest or concern. Identifying these commonalities can serve as a basis for finding solutions or working together toward a common goal. It can also humanize the difficult person, reminding you that they have their own motivations and desires. Building on shared interests can lead to more cooperative and less adversarial interactions.

In situations where direct communication with the difficult person is unproductive or impossible, seeking support from others can be a helpful coping mechanism. Talk to friends, family members, or colleagues who may have experience dealing with difficult people or who can provide emotional support and perspective. An outside viewpoint can occasionally throw light on viable solutions or different approaches to handling the circumstance. Additionally, when dealing with people who are especially difficult or when there is a major impact on your mental health, getting professional assistance from a therapist or counselor can be helpful. Practicing self-care is paramount when coping with difficult people. Dealing with challenging individuals can be emotionally draining and stressful. Engage in activities and practices that help you recharge and keep your mental and emotional well-being. This may include exercise, meditation, hobbies, spending time with loved ones, or seeking professional help when needed. Prioritizing self-care ensures that you have the resilience and emotional resources to handle difficult interactions effectively.

Lastly, it's essential to recognize when disengagement is the best coping mechanism. In some cases, despite your best efforts, interactions with a difficult person may remain unproductive or even harmful. Disengaging from such individuals can be a valid choice for self-preservation. It may mean limiting or ending the relationship, creating physical or emotional distance, or choosing to no longer engage in confrontational or fruitless conversations.

In conclusion, coping with difficult people is a challenge that many individuals face in various aspects of their lives.

Employing coping mechanisms such as active listening, empathy, setting boundaries, remaining calm, practicing assertiveness, depersonalizing behavior, finding common ground, seeking support, practicing self-care, and recognizing when disengagement is necessary can help individuals navigate these challenging interactions more effectively and with greater emotional well-being. Dealing with difficult people is not only about managing their behavior but also about protecting one's own mental and emotional health. Ultimately, effective coping mechanisms can lead to more constructive relationships and a higher quality of life.

Strategies for staying calm under pressure

Life often presents us with situations that require us to perform under pressure, whether it's a high-stakes presentation at work, a competitive sports event, a challenging exam, or a personal crisis. Being able to maintain composure under pressure is a useful skill that can have a big impact on our performance and general well-being. We are better able to think clearly, make wiser decisions, and control our emotions when we remain composed under pressure. This section will explore strategies and techniques for staying calm under pressure.

One of the fundamental strategies for staying calm under pressure is practicing mindfulness. Mindfulness involves paying full, non-judgmental attention to the present moment. It allows us to become aware of our thoughts, emotions, and physical sensations without reacting impulsively. By practicing mindfulness regularly, we develop the ability to stay grounded in the present, which can be immensely helpful in high-pressure situations. Deep breathing is an easy yet effective technique for reducing stress and staying calm. When we're under pressure, our bodies tend to respond with shallow, rapid breaths. Deep breathing involves taking slow, deliberate breaths, inhaling deeply through the nose, holding for a few seconds, and exhaling slowly through the mouth. This practice can activate the body's relaxation response, lower stress hormones, and help us regain a sense of calm.

Visualization is a powerful mental strategy for staying calm under pressure. Before a challenging event, take a few moments to visualize yourself performing successfully. Imagine the details—the sights, sounds, and feelings of success. This mental rehearsal can boost confidence as well as reduce anxiety. Athletes, in particular, often use visualization techniques to enhance their performance.

Another effective strategy is to break tasks into smaller, manageable steps. When faced with a daunting task or a tight deadline, it's easy to feel overwhelmed. Breaking the task into smaller, more achievable steps can make it feel less intimidating. By focusing on one step at a time, we can stay focused and reduce the pressure associated with the entire task.

Preparation is key to remaining calm under pressure. The more prepared we are, the more confident we feel. Whether it's studying for an exam, rehearsing a presentation, or practicing a skill, thorough preparation can boost our self-assurance and reduce anxiety. Knowing that we've put in the effort and are well-prepared can be a source of calm in high-pressure situations.

Positive self-talk is a cognitive technique that can help us stay calm under pressure. Pay attention to the way you speak to yourself when you're facing a stressful situation. Replace negative or self-critical thoughts with positive and affirming ones. Remind yourself of your strengths, past successes, and your ability to handle challenges. Positive self-talk can boost self-esteem and reduce self-doubt.

It's important to manage time effectively when facing pressure. Procrastination and last-minute rushing can significantly increase stress levels. To stay calm, create a realistic timeline for tasks and projects, and stick to it. Prioritize your work, break tasks into manageable chunks, and allocate sufficient time for each. The accumulation of pressure can be avoided with effective time management.

Exercise is a natural way to mitigate stress and maintain composure under pressure. Frequent exercise releases endorphins, which are organic mood enhancers. Exercises like yoga, jogging, or even a quick stroll can help lower stress and anxiety. It's essential to incorporate physical exercise into your routine to build resilience to pressure. Staying organized can also contribute to staying calm under pressure. A cluttered environment or disorganized workspaces can increase stress levels. Organize your physical space and create systems for managing tasks and responsibilities. When you know where things are and have a clear plan, you're less likely to feel overwhelmed. Seeking social support is another effective strategy for staying calm under pressure. Talking to friends, family members, or colleagues about your challenges and seeking their advice or emotional support can be comforting. Sometimes, simply sharing your feelings and concerns with someone you trust can lessen stress and provide a fresh perspective.

Another helpful strategy is to stay flexible and adapt to changing circumstances. Pressure often arises when unexpected changes or obstacles occur. Instead of resisting change, try to embrace it as an opportunity to learn and grow. Being flexible and adaptable can help you navigate unexpected challenges with a calm and resilient mindset.

Practice relaxation techniques regularly to build resilience to pressure. Techniques like guided imagery, progressive muscle relaxation, or mindfulness meditation can help you become more mindful of your body's stress response and learn to manage it effectively. These techniques can be particularly beneficial in high-pressure situations.

Remember that it's okay to take breaks and practice self-care. Pushing yourself to the limit without breaks can lead to burnout and increased stress. Taking short breaks to recharge, engaging in hobbies, or simply doing something you enjoy can help reduce stress and keep a sense of calm.

Finally, maintaining a sense of perspective is essential when facing pressure. Remind yourself that while the situation may feel urgent or critical at the moment, it is just one part of your life. Keep the bigger picture in mind and consider the long-term consequences. Often, this perspective can help reduce the perceived pressure of the moment.

In conclusion, staying calm under pressure is a skill that can be developed as well as honed with practice. By incorporating strategies such as mindfulness, deep breathing, visualization, task breakdown, preparation, positive self-talk, time management, physical exercise, organization, seeking social support, flexibility, relaxation techniques, self-care, and maintaining perspective, individuals can improve their ability to manage stress and perform effectively in challenging situations. Staying calm under pressure is not about eliminating stress but about learning to respond to it in a healthy and adaptive way. With these strategies, individuals can face pressure with resilience, confidence, and a sense of calm.

CHAPTER VI

Setting Boundaries

The importance of healthy boundaries

Healthy boundaries are the invisible lines that we draw around ourselves to define our emotional, physical, and psychological limits. They are the framework within which we interact with others, set expectations, and establish a sense of self-worth and autonomy. Healthy boundaries are fundamental to maintaining our well-being and fostering positive relationships with others. This section will explore the significance of healthy boundaries, the consequences of lacking them, and strategies for establishing and maintaining them.

Healthy boundaries are crucial because they serve as a safeguard for our emotional and mental health. They allow us to protect our inner world and maintain a sense of self. When we have healthy boundaries, we can differentiate between our emotions and the emotions of others. This emotional clarity is essential for maintaining a stable sense of self and preventing emotional enmeshment with others. Without healthy boundaries, we risk becoming emotionally overwhelmed and losing our individual identity in relationships.

Furthermore, healthy boundaries enable us to communicate our needs and preferences effectively. They provide a clear framework for expressing our desires, expectations, and limits to others. Doing so ensures that our needs are met, our values are respected, and our well-being is prioritized. When we fail to set and communicate boundaries, we may find ourselves in situations where our needs are neglected or overridden by others.

In personal relationships, healthy boundaries are essential for establishing and maintaining respect and mutual understanding. They define the rules of engagement, ensuring that both parties feel comfortable, safe, and valued. Respect for each other's boundaries leads to healthier and more fulfilling relationships, characterized by trust and open communication. In contrast, relationships where boundaries are routinely violated can become toxic and detrimental to one's mental and emotional health.

Healthy boundaries also play a vital role in professional settings. They help establish clear roles and responsibilities, which are essential for effective teamwork and productivity. Without clear boundaries in the workplace, confusion, conflicts, and burnout can occur. Individuals who fail to set boundaries may find themselves overworked, stressed, and unable to maintain a healthy work-life balance.

Furthermore, healthy boundaries protect us from exploitation and manipulation. They create a barrier against individuals who seek to take advantage of our kindness, generosity, or vulnerability. When we have strong boundaries, we can recognize when someone is crossing a line and take steps to protect ourselves from harm. Without healthy boundaries, we may become susceptible to manipulation or exploitation in various aspects of our lives.

One of the most significant consequences of lacking healthy boundaries is the risk of burnout. When we consistently overextend ourselves, say yes to every request, or fail to set limits on our time and energy, we are at risk of burning out physically and emotionally. Burnout can lead to exhaustion, stress-related illnesses, and a diminished sense of well-being. Setting and maintaining boundaries is a vital component of self-care and burnout prevention.

Additionally, a lack of healthy boundaries can lead to codependent or dysfunctional relationships. Codependency often arises when individuals have poor boundaries and become overly enmeshed in each other's lives. This can result in unhealthy patterns of enabling or relying excessively on others for validation and self-worth. Codependent relationships are marked by a lack of independence and can be emotionally draining and destructive.

Furthermore, without healthy boundaries, individuals may struggle with asserting themselves and saying no when necessary. This difficulty in setting limits can lead to feelings of powerlessness and resentment. People-pleasing behaviors, a common outcome of poor boundaries, can erode self-esteem and hinder personal growth. Learning to say no and assert one's needs is a vital aspect of self-empowerment.

Establishing and maintaining healthy boundaries requires self-awareness and self-compassion. It is essential to recognize our own needs, values, and limits before we can effectively communicate and enforce boundaries with others. Self-awareness allows us to understand what is acceptable and unacceptable to us, while self-compassion reminds us that it is okay to prioritize our well-being and set boundaries when necessary.

Effective communication is another critical component of healthy boundaries. It involves expressing our boundaries clearly, assertively, and respectfully. When setting boundaries, it is essential to use "I" statements to express our needs and feelings, rather than making accusatory or blaming statements. Effective communication can prevent misunderstandings and conflicts and foster mutual respect in relationships.

Taking care of oneself is essential to keeping appropriate boundaries. Maintaining our physical, emotional, and mental health gives us the fortitude and stamina to uphold boundaries on a regular basis. Self-care practices may include regular exercise, relaxation techniques, seeking therapy or counseling, and engaging in activities that bring joy and fulfillment.

Establishing boundaries is an ongoing process that may require practice and adjustment. It is essential to be consistent in enforcing boundaries and to reassess them when circumstances change. Boundaries are not rigid but can evolve over time as we gain a deeper understanding of ourselves and our needs.

In conclusion, healthy boundaries are a cornerstone of our emotional and mental well-being. They protect our sense of self, allow us to communicate our needs effectively, and promote respectful and fulfilling relationships. The consequences of lacking healthy boundaries can be detrimental to our physical as well as emotional health, leading to burnout, codependency, and dysfunction in relationships. Recognizing the importance of healthy boundaries and implementing strategies for setting and maintaining them is a crucial aspect of self-care and personal growth. It empowers us to live authentically, prioritize our well-being, and build healthier and more satisfying connections with others.

How to establish and communicate boundaries

In every aspect of our lives, boundaries are crucial in maintaining healthy relationships and personal well- being. Whether in our professional or personal lives, boundaries serve as the invisible lines that define what is acceptable and unacceptable behavior. They provide a sense of safety, respect, and balance in our interactions with others. This section explores the importance of establishing and effectively communicating boundaries, and it offers practical insights into how to do so.

To begin, it is essential to understand what boundaries are and why they matter. Boundaries are the limits we set for ourselves and others regarding what we are willing to tolerate, accept, or engage in. They can be physical, emotional, or interpersonal. For instance, a physical boundary might involve personal space, while an emotional boundary could relate to one's feelings and vulnerabilities. Establishing and communicating boundaries is crucial because they promote self-respect, prevent exploitation, and create a framework for healthy relationships.

The first stage in establishing boundaries is self-awareness. To set boundaries effectively, we must first identify our own needs, values, and limits. This self-reflection allows us to clarify what is important to us and what we are willing to compromise on. It is essential to recognize that boundaries are not fixed; they can evolve over time as our circumstances and priorities change. Therefore, continuous self-awareness is key to maintaining healthy boundaries.

Once we have a clear understanding of our own boundaries, the next step is communicating them to others. Effective communication is vital in ensuring that our boundaries are respected. It is important to express our needs and limits assertively and respectfully. Avoiding passive or aggressive communication styles is crucial. Instead, assertive communication involves clearly stating our boundaries while respecting the perspectives and feelings of others.

Setting boundaries also requires consistency. It is not enough to communicate our boundaries once and assume they will always be respected. People may forget or inadvertently cross our boundaries, so it is essential to reinforce them when necessary. Consistency sends a clear message that our boundaries are non-negotiable, fostering an environment of respect.

In professional settings, establishing boundaries can be particularly challenging. Work environments often blur the lines between personal and professional life, making it essential to define clear boundaries. For instance, one may need to communicate limits on working hours or the types of tasks they are willing to undertake. Failure to set such boundaries can lead to burnout and dissatisfaction. By clearly communicating limits to colleagues and supervisors, individuals can create a healthier work-life balance.

In personal relationships, boundaries are equally critical. Intimate partnerships, friendships, and family relationships all benefit from well-defined boundaries. Personal boundaries in relationships can encompass various aspects, such as physical intimacy, personal space, emotional availability, and communication preferences. Healthy relationships thrive when individuals feel safe and respected within them. By communicating their boundaries openly and honestly, individuals can build trust and intimacy in their personal connections.

Furthermore, it is essential to recognize that boundaries are not solely about setting limits on what we are not willing to accept; they also involve expressing our needs and desires. Effective boundary-setting involves a balance between asserting what we require and respecting the autonomy of others. It is a two-way process that encourages open dialogue and negotiation. When both parties in a relationship can communicate their boundaries and find common ground, the relationship becomes more resilient and fulfilling.

In addition to self-awareness, communication, and consistency, self-care is another crucial aspect of maintaining healthy boundaries. Setting boundaries should not be a one-sided endeavor where we prioritize the needs of others over our well-being. Self-care involves prioritizing our physical and emotional health, recognizing when we need to recharge, and saying no when necessary. It is only when we take care of ourselves that we can effectively set and enforce boundaries in our interactions with others.

In conclusion, establishing and communicating boundaries is a fundamental aspect of maintaining healthy relationships and personal well-being. Boundaries provide a framework for self-respect, prevent exploitation, and foster trust and respect in interactions with others. To establish boundaries effectively, one must start with self-awareness, communicate assertively and respectfully, remain consistent, and prioritize self-care. By doing so, individuals can create a harmonious balance between their own needs and the needs of those around them, leading to more fulfilling and satisfying relationships.

Dealing with boundary violations

In the complex web of human interactions, boundaries serve as the invisible barriers that protect our personal space, emotions, and well-being. Boundaries are essential for keeping healthy relationships and ensuring that we are treated with respect and dignity. However, despite our best efforts to establish and communicate boundaries, boundary violations can still occur. Dealing with these violations is a crucial skill that enables us to protect ourselves, maintain our self-respect, and foster healthier connections with others. This section explores the importance of addressing boundary violations and provides insights into effective strategies for dealing with them.

Boundary violations can take various forms, including physical, emotional, and interpersonal intrusions. In professional settings, they might involve colleagues overstepping personal space or exploiting one's time and resources. In personal relationships, boundary violations can manifest as emotional manipulation, invasion of privacy, or disrespect for one's feelings and autonomy. Regardless of the context, boundary violations can have negative consequences, such as erosion of trust, emotional distress, and damage to one's self-esteem.

The first step in dealing with boundary violations is recognizing them. Sometimes, individuals may not be fully aware that their boundaries have been crossed, especially if the violation is subtle or unintentional. Self-awareness plays a critical role in identifying when a boundary has been breached. It involves tuning into one's feelings and instincts to recognize discomfort, resentment, or unease in response to someone's actions or words. Trusting your instincts is essential, as they often serve as early warning signals of boundary violations. Once a boundary violation is recognized, the next step is to address it directly and assertively. This can be challenging, as many people fear confrontation or worry about damaging relationships. However, failing to address boundary violations can lead to ongoing discomfort and resentment. Assertive communication involves clearly and respectfully expressing your feelings and boundaries to the person who crossed them. It is crucial to use "I" statements to convey your perspective without blaming or accusing the other person. For example, saying, "I felt uncomfortable when you shared my personal information without my consent" is more effective than saying, "You shouldn't have shared my information."

It is important to remember that setting boundaries is not about changing others' behavior; it is about asserting your own needs and limits. When addressing boundary violations, it is possible that the other person may not even be aware of the impact of their actions. By communicating assertively, you provide them with an opportunity to understand your perspective and make amends. In some situations, this can lead to improved mutual understanding and a stronger relationship.

However, not all boundary violators will respond positively to assertive communication. Some individuals may become defensive, dismissive, or even hostile when confronted about their behavior. In such cases, it is essential to prioritize your own well-being and safety. You may need to distance yourself from the person or seek support from a trusted friend, family member, or professional. Protecting your boundaries should always be a priority, even if it means limiting or terminating a relationship that consistently disregards your limits and feelings.

In addition to assertive communication, setting consequences for boundary violations can be an effective strategy. Clearly communicate the consequences that will follow if the violations continue. These consequences should be proportionate to the severity and frequency of the violations. For example, if a colleague repeatedly interrupts your work without permission, you might explain that you will limit your availability for non-work-related interactions during specific hours to maintain focus and productivity.

Self-care is another crucial element of dealing with boundary violations. When our boundaries are violated, it can take an emotional toll on us. It is essential to prioritize self-care to help restore our emotional well-being. Self-care can involve practices such as mindfulness, meditation, exercise, or seeking professional support through therapy or counseling. By taking care of ourselves, we become more resilient in the face of boundary violations and better equipped to address them effectively.

Furthermore, learning from boundary violations can be an opportunity for personal growth and self-discovery.

Reflect on the experience and take into account what you can learn from it. Did you communicate your boundaries clearly? Were there signs of discomfort that you ignored? Is there a pattern of boundary violations in your relationships that you need to address? Self-reflection can lead to a deeper understanding of your own needs and boundaries, allowing you to set them more effectively in the future.

In conclusion, dealing with boundary violations is an essential skill for keeping healthy relationships and personal well-being. Recognizing violations, addressing them assertively, setting consequences, prioritizing self-care, and learning from the experience are all valuable strategies for dealing with boundary violations effectively. It is important to remember that boundaries are a fundamental aspect of self-respect and maintaining healthy connections with others. By addressing violations assertively and compassionately, we can protect our boundaries and foster more respectful and fulfilling relationships.

CHAPTER VII

Strategies for Specific Types of Difficult People

Dealing with aggressive individuals

Interacting with aggressive individuals can be challenging and even intimidating. Aggression can manifest in various forms, including verbal outbursts, physical confrontations, or hostile behavior. Whether it occurs in a personal or professional setting, knowing how to deal with aggressive individuals effectively is a valuable skill that can diffuse tense situations, protect personal safety, and foster better communication. This section explores the importance of understanding and addressing aggression and provides insights into strategies for dealing with aggressive individuals.

First and foremost, it is crucial to recognize the different forms of aggression. Verbal aggression involves hurtful words, insults, threats, or shouting. Physical aggression includes actions such as pushing, hitting, or any form of physical harm. Passive-aggressive behavior involves indirect expressions of hostility or resistance, such as sarcasm, backhanded compliments, or deliberate procrastination. Understanding these variations of aggression helps in identifying and addressing them effectively.

Personal safety should be a top priority in any interaction with an aggressive individual. If you feel physically threatened or unsafe, it is essential to remove yourself from the situation immediately and seek assistance from authorities or security personnel. Physical safety should never be compromised when dealing with aggression.

When it comes to addressing verbal aggression, it is important to remain calm and composed. Responding with anger or aggression in return often escalates the situation. Instead, active listening can be a valuable tool. Give the person an opportunity to express their feelings and concerns. Show empathy by acknowledging their emotions, even if you don't agree with their perspective. Statements like "I understand you're upset" or "I hear that you're frustrated" can help de-escalate tension.

Moreover, setting boundaries is critical when dealing with aggressive individuals. Clearly and assertively communicate your own boundaries and expectations for respectful behavior. For example, you might say, "I'm willing to discuss this matter with you, but I won't tolerate shouting or insults. Let's have a respectful conversation." Setting boundaries helps establish a framework for respectful communication.

In situations where physical aggression is a concern, creating physical distance is essential for safety. Maintain a safe distance from the aggressive person and position yourself near exits or open spaces. If possible, have a colleague or friend present as a witness and for support. Avoid physically confronting the aggressive individual unless it is absolutely necessary for self-defense.

Maintaining open body language and avoiding sudden or threatening movements is also helpful. Keep your hands visible and avoid gestures that may be perceived as confrontational. Speak in a calm and even tone to de-escalate the situation. Avoid arguing or engaging in a power struggle, as this can further provoke aggression.

In cases of passive-aggressive behavior, addressing the issue directly can be effective. Express your concerns calmly and assertively. For example, you might say, "I noticed that you seem upset, but your sarcasm makes it difficult for us to have a productive conversation. Can we discuss this issue openly?" Passive-aggressive individuals may not be aware of how their behavior affects others, so open communication can lead to better understanding.

In some situations, involving a mediator or authority figure can help resolve conflicts with aggressive individuals. Mediation offers a neutral third party who can facilitate communication and guide the conversation toward a resolution. In workplace settings, HR professionals or supervisors often serve as mediators. In personal conflicts, a trusted friend or family member can fulfill this role.

It is essential to document incidents of aggression, especially in professional settings. Keep a record of dates, times, locations, and descriptions of aggressive behavior. This documentation can be valuable if further action, such as reporting the behavior to superiors or authorities, becomes necessary. Having evidence of the aggression can strengthen your case and protect your rights.

Furthermore, it is essential to seek support and guidance when dealing with aggressive individuals. Consult with family members, trusted friends, or colleagues who can provide emotional support and advice. If you feel overwhelmed or unable to handle the situation on your own, consider seeking professional help, such as counseling or therapy, to develop coping strategies and communication skills.

In conclusion, dealing with aggressive individuals requires a combination of strategies aimed at ensuring personal safety, maintaining composure, setting boundaries, and promoting open communication. Recognizing the different forms of aggression, knowing when to involve authorities or mediators, and seeking support from trusted individuals are all essential aspects of effectively handling aggressive behavior. While it can be challenging, addressing aggression with a calm and assertive approach can lead to de-escalation and, ideally, a resolution that promotes healthier interactions and relationships.

Handling passive-aggressive behavior

Passive-aggressive behavior is a challenging and often subtle form of interpersonal communication. Unlike overt aggression, passive-aggressive behavior is indirect and can be difficult to recognize. It involves expressing negative feelings or resistance in a covert manner, such as sarcasm, procrastination, or backhanded compliments. Dealing with passive-aggressive conduct can be frustrating and confusing, but it is essential to address it effectively to maintain healthy relationships and promote open communication. This section explores the nature of passive-aggressive behavior, its impact, and strategies for handling it constructively.

Understanding passive-aggressive behavior begins with recognizing its various forms. One common manifestation is sarcasm, where individuals use humor or witty remarks to convey criticism or frustration indirectly. For example, instead of expressing their disagreement openly, a passive-aggressive person might make a sarcastic comment such as, "Oh, great idea! That worked out so well last time." Another form of passive-aggression is procrastination, where individuals delay tasks or responsibilities as a way to resist demands or express resentment. Additionally, subtle insults or backhanded compliments can be used to disguise negative feelings. Recognizing these patterns is crucial for identifying passive-aggressive behavior.

Passive-aggressive behavior can have a significant effect on relationships and communication. It develops an atmosphere of tension and mistrust, as the true intentions of the passive-aggressive individual are often hidden. Moreover, passive-aggressive behavior can hinder effective problem-solving and conflict resolution, as it avoids direct and honest communication. This can lead to unresolved issues and lingering resentment, eroding the quality of relationships over time.

To effectively handle passive-aggressive behavior, it is important to adopt a proactive approach. Start by addressing the behavior directly but calmly. Reacting angrily or frustratedly should be avoided as this can make things worse. Instead, use assertive communication to express your feelings and concerns. For example, you might say, "I noticed that you often use sarcasm when we discuss this topic, and it makes it challenging for us to have a productive conversation. Can we talk openly about our concerns?"

Active listening is another valuable tool when dealing with passive-aggressive behavior. Encourage the passive-aggressive individual to express their thoughts and feelings openly, even if they are using indirect or sarcastic language. Show empathy by acknowledging their emotions, and try to understand their perspective. Sometimes, passive-aggressive behavior is a result of unexpressed frustrations or unresolved issues that need to be addressed.

Setting clear boundaries is essential when handling passive-aggressive behavior. Clearly communicate your expectations for respectful communication and behavior. Let the passive-aggressive person know that sarcasm, insults, or other covert forms of communication are not acceptable. Be specific about the behavior you find problematic and express your desire for more direct and open communication.

It is also important to remain patient and persistent when dealing with passive-aggressive individuals. Changing behavior patterns can take time, and the passive-aggressive person may not be aware of the impact of their actions. By consistently addressing the behavior and reinforcing your boundaries, you can encourage more constructive communication over time.

In some cases, seeking the assistance of a mediator or therapist can be beneficial when dealing with persistent passive-aggressive behavior. A mediator can provide a neutral and objective perspective and facilitate communication between parties. Therapy can help individuals comprehend the underlying causes of their passive-aggressive behavior and develop healthier communication skills.

When addressing passive-aggressive behavior, it is important to avoid falling into the same patterns of behavior yourself. Responding with passive-aggressiveness or hostility only perpetuates the cycle of unproductive communication. Instead, model the kind of open, direct, and respectful communication you would like to see from the other person.

Self-care is a crucial component of dealing with passive-aggressive behavior. It can be emotionally draining to navigate the challenges of passive-aggressive interactions. Practicing self-care involves taking time to recharge, engage in activities that bring you joy as well as relaxation, and seeking support from trusted friends or professionals if necessary. Maintaining your own emotional well-being is essential when handling passive-aggressive behavior.

In conclusion, handling passive-aggressive behavior requires patience, assertiveness, and a commitment to open communication. Understanding the nature of passive-aggressive behavior, recognizing its impact, and using proactive strategies to address it are key steps in promoting healthier interactions and relationships. By addressing passive-aggressive behavior directly, setting clear boundaries, and practicing active listening, individuals can work toward resolving conflicts and fostering more productive and respectful communication with others.

Navigating narcissistic personalities

Dealing with narcissistic personalities can be a challenging and often emotionally draining experience. A personality trait known as narcissism is defined by an exaggerated sense of one's own importance, an overwhelming need for admiration and attention, and a deficiency of empathy for other people. Interacting with individuals who exhibit narcissistic traits can be complicated, whether it occurs in personal relationships, the workplace, or social settings. This section explores the nature of narcissistic personalities, the impact they can have on those around them, and strategies for effectively navigating interactions with such individuals.

Understanding narcissistic personalities begins with recognizing their defining characteristics. Narcissists often display a grandiose sense of self, believing they are superior to others and that they are deserving of special treatment. They may constantly seek validation and admiration from others while lacking empathy for the feelings and needs of those around them. Additionally, narcissists may exhibit a sense of entitlement, manipulation, and a tendency to exploit others for personal gain. Recognizing these traits is crucial for identifying narcissistic individuals.

The impact of interacting with narcissistic personalities can be profound and negative. In personal relationships, such as partnerships or friendships, narcissistic individuals may dominate conversations, dismiss others' feelings, and expect constant attention and praise. Their lack of empathy can lead to emotional neglect and manipulation. In professional settings, narcissists may create toxic environments by prioritizing their own success over teamwork and disregarding the contributions of others. Their constant need for validation can lead to favoritism and unequal treatment.

When navigating interactions with narcissistic individuals, it is essential to prioritize self-care. Dealing with their behavior can be emotionally exhausting, so it is crucial to engage in practices that promote your own well-being. Self-care can involve setting boundaries, seeking support from trusted friends or professionals, and engaging in activities that bring you joy and relaxation. Maintaining your emotional health is key when dealing with narcissistic personalities.

Establishing and maintaining clear boundaries is fundamental when interacting with narcissistic individuals. Communicate your expectations clearly for respectful behavior and assertively express your own needs and limits. Narcissists may push boundaries, so it is important to reinforce them consistently. Be prepared for resistance, as narcissists often react negatively to boundaries, but holding firm is essential for your well-being.

Effective communication is another important strategy when navigating interactions with narcissistic individuals. While it may be challenging, strive to maintain calm and assertive communication. Avoid becoming emotionally reactive or defensive, as this can fuel conflict. Use "I" statements to express your feelings as well as concerns. For example, say, "I feel unheard and disrespected when you interrupt me during our conversations. I would appreciate it if we could have a more equal exchange."

Active listening can also be a useful tool when dealing with narcissistic personalities. Encourage the narcissist to express their thoughts and feelings, even if they are self-centered. Show empathy by acknowledging their emotions and concerns, as this can help de-escalate tension and foster a more open dialogue. Remember that narcissistic individuals may have deep-seated insecurities beneath their grandiose exterior, and active listening can reveal underlying issues.

Maintaining a support system is crucial when navigating interactions with narcissistic personalities. Seek assistance and guidance from trusted friends, family members, or colleagues who can give emotional support and perspective. Narcissists often manipulate and gaslight their targets, making it essential to have a reliable support network that can help you see through their tactics.

It is important to avoid trying to change or "fix" narcissistic individuals. Narcissism is a complex personality trait that often resists change, as narcissists rarely see their behavior as problematic. Instead, focus on managing your reactions and responses to their behavior. Accept that you may not be able to change them, but you can control how you engage with them.

In some cases, professional assistance, such as therapy or counseling, may be helpful when dealing with narcissistic individuals, especially in personal relationships. A therapist can help you create coping strategies, set healthy boundaries, and navigate the emotional challenges that arise in interactions with narcissists. Therapy can also provide a secure space to explore your own feelings and needs.

In conclusion, navigating interactions with narcissistic personalities requires self-awareness, assertive communication, boundary-setting, and a commitment to self-care. Recognizing the defining traits of narcissism, understanding its impact, and implementing strategies to protect your well-being are all essential steps when dealing with narcissistic individuals. By maintaining clear boundaries, seeking support, and focusing on your own emotional health, you can navigate these challenging interactions with greater resilience and effectiveness. Remember that, ultimately, you have the power to control your responses and protect your own well-being when dealing with narcissistic personalities.

Coping with manipulative people

Dealing with manipulative individuals can be a complex and emotionally challenging experience. Manipulation involves the use of deceit, cunning tactics, and emotional control to achieve personal gain at the expense of others. Manipulative people often employ various strategies to influence and control those around them, whether in personal relationships, the workplace, or social settings. This section explores the nature of manipulative behavior, the emotional toll it can take, and strategies for effectively coping with manipulative individuals.

Understanding manipulative behavior begins with recognizing its characteristics and tactics. Manipulators often employ tactics such as guilt-tripping, gaslighting, playing the victim, or withholding information to gain power and control. They may exploit others' emotions, vulnerabilities, and trust to achieve their goals. Manipulators are skilled at concealing their true intentions and portraying themselves as innocent or helpful, making it challenging to identify their behavior.

The emotional toll of interacting with manipulative individuals can be profound. Victims of manipulation often experience feelings of confusion, frustration, self-doubt, and anxiety. Manipulators can erode self-esteem, create a sense of powerlessness, and foster a climate of distrust and paranoia. It is common for victims to question their judgment and become entangled in a web of lies and deceit spun by the manipulator.

When coping with manipulative individuals, it is crucial to prioritize self-care. Dealing with their behavior can be emotionally exhausting, so taking steps to maintain your own well-being is essential. Engage in practices that promote emotional resilience, such as mindfulness, meditation, or exercise. Seek help from trusted family members, friends, or professionals who can give emotional validation and perspective.

Establishing and maintaining clear boundaries is fundamental when dealing with manipulative individuals. Manipulators often exploit weaknesses in boundaries, so it is crucial to communicate your expectations for respectful behavior assertively. Be prepared for pushback, as manipulators may resist boundaries, but holding firm is essential for your emotional and psychological well-being.

Effective communication is another key strategy when coping with manipulative individuals. While it may be challenging, strive to maintain calm and assertive communication. Avoid becoming emotionally reactive or defensive, as this can feed into the manipulator's tactics. Use the "I" statements to express your feelings and concerns directly. For example, say, "I feel uncomfortable when you use guilt-tripping to get your way. I would appreciate it if we could have a more honest and open conversation."

Dealing with manipulative people can also benefit from the use of active listening techniques. Encourage the manipulator to express their thoughts and feelings, even if they are using manipulative tactics. Show empathy by acknowledging their emotions and concerns, as this can help de-escalate tension and create a space for more open dialogue. Remember that manipulators often have their own insecurities and vulnerabilities, which may be driving their behavior.

Maintaining a support system is crucial when coping with manipulative individuals. Seek assistance and guidance from trusted family members, friends, or colleagues who can give emotional support and perspective. Manipulative individuals may attempt to isolate their victims, making it vital to have a reliable support network that can help you see through their tactics and offer validation and guidance.

It is essential to avoid engaging in power struggles or attempts to change the manipulative individual. Manipulators are often resistant to change and may become more entrenched in their behavior when confronted directly. Instead, focus on managing your reactions and responses to their tactics. Accept that you may not be able to change them, but you can control how you engage with them.

In some cases, seeking professional assistance, such as therapy or counseling, may be beneficial when coping with manipulative individuals, especially in personal relationships. A therapist can help you establish coping strategies, set healthy boundaries, and navigate the emotional challenges that arise in interactions with manipulators. Therapy can provide a secure and supportive space to explore your feelings, needs, and options for managing manipulative behavior.

In conclusion, coping with manipulative individuals requires self-awareness, assertive communication, boundary-setting, and a commitment to self-care. Recognizing the tactics and characteristics of manipulative behavior, understanding its emotional toll, and implementing strategies to protect your well-being are all essential steps when dealing with manipulative individuals. By maintaining clear boundaries, seeking support, and focusing on your own emotional health, you can navigate these challenging interactions with greater resilience and effectiveness. Remember that, ultimately, you have the power to control your responses and protect your own well-being when dealing with manipulative individuals.

Addressing toxic relationships

Toxic relationships are characterized by consistent patterns of behavior that cause harm, distress, and negativity to one or both individuals involved. These relationships can manifest in different forms, such as romantic partnerships, friendships, family connections, or workplace dynamics. Dealing with toxic relationships can be emotionally draining and detrimental to one's overall well-being. However, recognizing the signs, understanding the impact, and taking proactive steps to address toxicity are essential for personal growth, emotional health, and the possibility of either healing or moving on. This section explores the nature of toxic relationships, their impact, and strategies for effectively addressing them.

Recognizing toxic relationships begins with identifying the signs and patterns of toxic behavior. Toxic individuals often display behaviors such as manipulation, control, emotional abuse, excessive criticism, disrespect, or a lack of empathy. They may create an atmosphere of constant negativity, drama, and conflict. It is crucial to trust your instincts and recognize when a relationship consistently brings more harm than joy.

The impact of toxic relationships can be profound and far-reaching. They can erode self-esteem, create emotional turmoil, and contribute to stress, anxiety, and depression. Toxic relationships can isolate individuals from their support systems, making it challenging to seek help or perspective from others. They can also hinder personal growth and prevent individuals from pursuing their goals and dreams.

When addressing toxic relationships, the first step is acknowledging the situation and accepting that the relationship is harmful. Denial or minimization of toxicity can prolong the pain and prevent necessary action. Once you recognize the toxicity, it is essential to prioritize your emotional and psychological well-being.

Establishing boundaries is crucial when handling unhealthy partnerships. Express your demands for appropriate behavior in a clear and concise manner, and stand up for your own needs and boundaries. Be prepared for resistance or backlash, as toxic individuals may not react positively to boundaries, but maintaining them is essential for your well-being.

Effective communication is another critical strategy when addressing toxic relationships. Calm and assertive communication can help express your feelings, concerns, and boundaries. Avoid becoming emotionally reactive or defensive, as this can escalate conflict. Use "I" statements to express your perspective directly, focusing on your own feelings and needs rather than attacking or blaming the other person.

Active listening is valuable when dealing with toxic relationships. Encourage the toxic individual to express their thoughts and feelings, even if they are critical or manipulative. Show empathy by acknowledging their emotions and concerns. Sometimes, toxic behavior can stem from unresolved issues or unmet needs, and active listening may reveal underlying issues.

Maintaining a support system is essential when addressing toxic relationships. Seek assistance and guidance from trusted friends, family members, or professionals who can offer emotional support and perspective. Toxic individuals often isolate their victims, making it vital to have a reliable support network that can help you see through the toxicity and offer validation and guidance.

It is essential to avoid engaging in power struggles or attempts to change the toxic individual. Toxic behavior often resists change, and efforts to confront or control it may lead to further harm or emotional exhaustion. Instead, focus on managing your own reactions as well as responses to the toxic behavior. Accept that you may not be able to change the other person, but you can control how you engage with them.

In some situations, ending the toxic relationship may be the most appropriate course of action. This decision can be particularly challenging in long-term relationships or with family members, but it is crucial to prioritize your well-being as well as emotional health. Seeking professional guidance, like therapy or counseling, can provide support and guidance during the process of ending a toxic relationship.
In other situations, if both individuals are willing to work on the relationship, couples or family therapy may be a valuable option. Therapy can help determine and address the underlying issues contributing to toxicity and provide tools for healthier communication and conflict resolution.

In conclusion, addressing toxic relationships requires self-awareness, assertive communication, boundary-setting, and a commitment to self-care. Recognizing the signs of toxicity, understanding its impact, and implementing strategies to protect your well-being are all essential steps when dealing with toxic relationships. By maintaining clear boundaries, seeking support, and focusing on your own emotional health, you can navigate these challenging situations with greater resilience and effectiveness. Remember that, ultimately, you have the power to control your responses and prioritize your own well-being when addressing toxic relationships.

Chapter VIII

Workplace Dynamics

Managing difficult colleagues or superiors

In the complex landscape of the workplace, interactions with colleagues and superiors are an inevitable part of professional life. While many of these interactions are positive and collaborative, there are times when individuals find themselves dealing with difficult colleagues or superiors. These difficult relationships can stem from various factors, including conflicting personalities, communication challenges, or differences in work styles. Managing these relationships effectively is essential for maintaining a productive and harmonious work environment. This section explores strategies and approaches for managing difficult colleagues or superiors, with a focus on fostering open communication, setting boundaries, and seeking resolution.

The first step in managing difficult colleagues or superiors is recognizing the signs of a challenging relationship. Difficult individuals may display behaviors such as condescension, passive-aggressiveness, micromanagement, or resistance to feedback. They may create tension, conflict, or stress within the workplace. Identifying these signs early on allows individuals to address problems before they escalate and negatively impact job satisfaction and productivity.

Effective communication is paramount when dealing with difficult colleagues or superiors.Finding common ground, addressing issues, and clearing up misunderstandings can all be facilitated by open and honest communication. Even if you disagree with the other person's viewpoint, begin by paying attention to what they have to say. Make sure you understand their goals and motivations by asking clarifying questions. Often, difficult behavior can stem from miscommunication or differing expectations.

When communicating with a difficult colleague or superior, it is necessary to remain calm and composed. Emotions can run high in challenging situations, but responding with anger or defensiveness can exacerbate the conflict. Use assertive communication to express your thoughts as well as feelings respectfully. Avoid accusatory language and focus on specific behaviors or issues that need addressing. For example, instead of saying, "You're always so controlling," you might say, "I've noticed that you provide detailed feedback on my work, and it feels like you don't trust my judgment. Can we discuss how we can work together more effectively?"

Setting boundaries is crucial for managing difficult relationships in the workplace. Communicate your expectations clearly for respectful behavior and assertively express your own needs and limits. For example, if a colleague frequently interrupts your work, you might say, "I need focused time to complete my tasks. Can we establish specific times for meetings or discussions to minimize disruptions?" Setting boundaries helps create a framework for more productive and harmonious interactions.

In some cases, it may be necessary to involve a third party to mediate or facilitate communication. This can be specifically helpful when dealing with difficult superiors or when conflicts are deeply ingrained. A mediator, such as a supervisor, HR professional, or an external consultant, can provide an impartial perspective and guide the conversation toward resolution. Mediation can be a constructive way to address issues and find common ground.

Furthermore, seeking feedback and self-reflection can be valuable when managing difficult colleagues or superiors. Consider gathering feedback from trusted colleagues or mentors to gain insights into your own communication style and how it may contribute to the challenges you face. Self-reflection allows you to examine your own behavior and identify areas for improvement. It is important to recognize that managing difficult relationships is a two-way process, and personal growth and self-awareness are key components of the solution.

When all else fails, and the situation remains unmanageable or escalates, individuals may need to consider seeking assistance from higher management or HR departments. Documenting specific instances of difficult behavior and maintaining a record of communication attempts can be helpful in presenting a case for intervention. However, involving higher authorities should be a last resort, as it can have potential repercussions and should only be pursued when other avenues have been exhausted.

In some situations, individuals may need to evaluate whether it is in their best interest to continue working in an environment with consistently difficult colleagues or superiors. While leaving a job is a significant decision, it may be necessary for personal well-being and career growth. Prioritizing one's mental and emotional health is paramount, and no job is worth enduring chronic stress or mistreatment.

In conclusion, managing difficult colleagues or superiors requires a combination of strategies, including effective communication, boundary-setting, seeking feedback, and, when necessary, seeking outside mediation or intervention. Recognizing the signs of a challenging relationship and addressing issues proactively are essential steps in finding resolution. Difficult relationships can be challenging, but with patience, self-awareness, and a commitment to open communication, individuals can navigate these situations with greater effectiveness and resilience, ultimately contributing to a healthier and a more productive work environment. Remember that managing difficult relationships is a skill that can be developed and refined over time, benefiting both your professional growth and your overall job satisfaction.

Conflict resolution in the workplace

Conflict is an inherent part of the workplace, arising from diverse personalities, competing priorities, and differing opinions. When managed effectively, conflict can result in positive outcomes, such as improved communication, enhanced creativity, and better decision-making. However, unresolved or poorly handled conflicts can escalate, resulting in strained relationships, decreased morale, and reduced productivity. Effective conflict resolution is an essential skill for keeping a healthy and productive work environment. This section explores the nature of workplace conflict, the impact it can have, and strategies for resolving conflicts constructively.

Workplace conflict can take many forms, including disagreements over tasks or responsibilities, interpersonal clashes, misunderstandings, or differences in work styles. Conflict often arises from unmet expectations, miscommunication, or a lack of clarity about the roles as well as responsibilities. It is essential to recognize that conflict is not inherently negative; it can serve as a catalyst for growth and improvement when managed constructively.

One of the key impacts of unresolved workplace conflict is a decline in employee morale and job satisfaction. When individuals feel that their concerns are ignored or that conflicts persist without resolution, they may become disengaged, demotivated, and disheartened. This can result in reduced productivity, higher turnover rates, and a negative work atmosphere. Effective conflict resolution is vital for addressing these issues and fostering a more positive workplace culture.

The first stage in effective conflict resolution is acknowledging the existence of the conflict. Ignoring or avoiding conflicts can lead to their escalation and exacerbation of the issues. Promote an open communication and create a secure space for employees to express their worries without fear of reprisal. When conflicts are addressed promptly, they are more likely to be resolved positively.

Active listening is a fundamental skill in conflict resolution. When individuals feel heard and understood, they are more willing to engage in the resolution process. Listen attentively to each party involved, seeking to understand their perspectives, feelings, and underlying interests. Avoid interrupting or jumping to conclusions; but rather, ask clarifying questions to guarantee a comprehensive understanding.

In many workplace conflicts, emotions can run high, and individuals may become emotionally charged. It is necessary to stay calm and composed when facilitating conflict resolution. Emphasize the importance of respectful communication and set ground rules for the discussion to ensure that it remains constructive and focused on the issues at hand.

Seeking common ground is a critical component of resolving workplace conflicts. Encourage individuals to identify shared goals or interests that can serve as a basis for finding solutions. By focusing on common objectives, conflicting parties can shift their perspective from a win-lose mentality to a win-win approach, where both parties can benefit.

Problem-solving and negotiation skills play a significant role in conflict resolution. Encourage individuals to brainstorm solutions and generate options for resolving the conflict. Emphasize the importance of compromising and finding mutually acceptable solutions. Explore different alternatives and evaluate the potential outcomes of each.

Mediation can be a valuable equipment for resolving complex or deeply ingrained conflicts in the workplace. A neutral third party, often a manager, HR professional, or an external mediator, can facilitate the resolution process. Mediators can help individuals express their concerns, guide the discussion toward constructive solutions, and ensure that the process remains fair and impartial.

It is important to document the outcomes of conflict resolution discussions and any agreed-upon actions or solutions. This documentation serves as a reference point for future reference and accountability. Having a record of the resolution can also help prevent conflicts from resurfacing and provide a basis for evaluating the effectiveness of the chosen solutions.

Follow-up is an often-overlooked aspect of conflict resolution. After a conflict has been resolved, periodically check in with the individuals involved to ensure that the resolution is working effectively. Address any novel concerns or issues that may arise as a result of the initial conflict. Open communication and ongoing support are essential for maintaining a conflict-free work environment.

In some cases, workplace conflicts may be indicative of deeper organizational issues. It is crucial to consider whether systemic problems, such as unclear policies, inadequate communication channels, or a toxic culture, are contributing to conflicts. Addressing these underlying issues is essential for preventing future conflicts and creating a healthier work environment.

In conclusion, conflict resolution in the workplace is a critical skill for maintaining a productive and harmonious work environment. Recognizing the existence of conflicts, promoting open communication, and actively listening are essential steps in addressing conflicts constructively. By focusing on common ground, problem-solving, and negotiation, individuals and organizations can navigate conflicts effectively and foster a positive workplace culture. Remember that conflict resolution is a continuous process that needs commitment and effort, but the benefits of a conflict-free and collaborative work environment are well worth the investment.

Strategies for a harmonious work environment

A harmonious work environment is essential for the well-being and productivity of employees, as well as also the overall success of an organization. In a harmonious workplace, employees feel respected, valued, as well as motivated, resulting in increased job satisfaction and better performance. While challenges and conflicts can arise in any workplace, there are effective strategies that can be implemented to foster harmony, collaboration, and a positive atmosphere. This section explores key strategies for creating and maintaining a harmonious work environment, with a focus on communication, respect, work-life balance, and conflict resolution.

Effective communication is at the core of a harmonious work environment. Open and transparent communication helps employees understand their roles, expectations, and responsibilities. It also allows for the free exchange of ideas, feedback, and concerns. Employers should encourage regular and meaningful communication between team members, supervisors, and departments. Regular team meetings, one-on-one check-ins, and clear communication channels can facilitate information sharing and collaboration.

Respect for all employees, regardless of their role or position, is fundamental to a harmonious workplace. Respect involves treating colleagues with kindness, consideration, and professionalism. Employers should encourage a culture of respect by setting clear expectations for respectful behavior and addressing any instances of disrespect promptly. Respect also extends to diversity and inclusion, recognizing and valuing differences in backgrounds, perspectives, and experiences.

Work-life balance is crucial for keeping a harmonious work environment. Employees who have the flexibility to manage their workloads and personal lives are generally more satisfied and productive. Employers should encourage work-life balance by providing flexible scheduling options, remote work opportunities when feasible, and paid time off. It is also essential to establish boundaries to prevent overworking and burnout.

Conflict resolution is an integral part of creating and maintaining a harmonious work environment. Conflicts and disagreements are unavoidable in any workplace, but how they are managed can impact overall harmony. Employers should provide training in conflict resolution and establish clear procedures for addressing conflicts. Encourage employees to communicate openly about conflicts and provide a safe space for them to seek resolution. Mediation or involvement of HR professionals can be beneficial for addressing complex or ongoing conflicts.

Harmony at work can be greatly enhanced by showing appreciation and recognition for one another. Employee engagement and job satisfaction are positively correlated with feelings of value and appreciation. Employers should regularly acknowledge and celebrate the achievements and contributions of their employees. This can include verbal recognition, awards, bonuses, or other forms of appreciation. Recognizing employees' efforts and successes can boost morale and motivation.

Empowerment and involvement in decision-making processes can contribute to a harmonious work environment. Employees who have a voice in shaping their work and workplace are more likely to feel invested in their roles. Employers should involve employees in decision-making when appropriate, seek their input and feedback, and give opportunities for them to contribute to the organization's goals and direction. Empowered employees are often more motivated and committed to their work.

Professional development and growth opportunities are vital for employee satisfaction and harmony in the workplace. Employees who see a path for advancement and skill development are more likely to be engaged and committed to their careers. Employers should provide training, mentorship programs, and opportunities for skill enhancement and career advancement. Investing in employee growth not only benefits individuals but also the organization as a whole.

A harmonious work environment also depends on a safe and healthy workplace. Employers have a responsibility to guarantee the physical and emotional well-being of their employees. This entails providing a safe working environment, addressing health and safety concerns promptly, and offering resources for mental health and well-being. Employees should feel that their physical and emotional health is a priority for their organization.

Flexibility and adaptability are key aspects of maintaining a harmonious work environment, especially in a rapidly changing world. Employers should be open to accommodating changing needs and circumstances, such as those brought about by technological advancements or external events like the COVID-19 pandemic. The ability to adapt to new working conditions, embrace new technologies, and support employees through transitions can contribute to a harmonious and resilient workplace.

In conclusion, a harmonious work environment is essential for the well-being, satisfaction, and productivity of employees. Effective communication, respect, work-life balance, conflict resolution, recognition, empowerment, professional development, safety, and adaptability are key strategies for creating and maintaining harmony at work. Employers are significant in fostering a positive workplace culture, but it is a collective effort that involves all members of the organization. By implementing these strategies, organizations can create an environment where employees thrive, collaborate, and contribute to their fullest potential.

CHAPTER IX

Family and Personal Relationships

Managing difficult family members

Families are a source of love, support, and connection but can also be a breeding ground for conflicts, tensions, and challenging dynamics. Dealing with difficult family members is a common experience many individuals face at some point. These challenges can arise from differing personalities, unresolved past issues, or clashing values and beliefs. Navigating such relationships can be emotionally taxing, but it is crucial for maintaining family bonds and personal well-being. This section explores strategies for managing difficult family members, focusing on communication, setting boundaries, empathy, and seeking outside support.

Effective communication is the foundation of managing difficult family members. Open and honest dialogue is necessary for understanding each other's perspectives and finding common ground. When conflicts or tensions arise, addressing them calmly and assertively, without resorting to aggressive or confrontational language is important. Active listening is equally crucial; it involves giving the other person your full attention, showing empathy, and striving to understand their point of view. By actively listening and communicating respectfully, you can create a more conducive environment for resolving differences and improving your relationship with difficult family members.

Setting boundaries is another key strategy for managing difficult family members. Boundaries help protect your emotional well-being and establish clear guidelines for how you want to be treated. It is essential to communicate your boundaries constantly and assertively. For example, suppose a family member frequently criticizes your choices or invades your privacy. In that case, you might say, "I appreciate your concern, but I would like you to respect my decisions and privacy." Setting and maintaining boundaries may require time and persistence, but it is crucial for maintaining a healthy relationship with challenging family members.

Empathy is a potent tool when dealing with difficult family members. Empathizing with their feelings and perspective can help you understand their motivations and behavior. Try to put yourself in their shoes and consider their experiences and emotions. Often, difficult family members may be dealing with their struggles, insecurities, or unresolved issues. By showing empathy, you can develop a more compassionate and understanding atmosphere, which can pave the way for better communication and resolution of conflicts.

Seeking outside support can be invaluable when managing difficult family members. Sometimes, the dynamics within a family can be deeply ingrained, making it challenging to address issues on your own. Professional help, like family therapy or counseling, can offer a secure and neutral space to explore and work through complex family dynamics. A trained therapist can facilitate communication, mediate conflicts, and provide strategies for managing difficult family members more effectively.

It is essential to exercise self-care when dealing with challenging family members. The emotional toll of managing conflicts and tensions can be draining, so it is crucial to prioritize your own well-being. Engage in self-care practices that promote emotional resilience, such as exercise, meditation, or seeking support from friends or a therapist. Maintaining mental as well as emotional health is vital for managing difficult family members without sacrificing your well-being.

In some cases, it may be necessary to limit or adjust your interactions with difficult family members. While it is essential to strive for resolution and understanding, there may be situations where maintaining distance or creating space is the healthiest option. This does not necessarily mean cutting off all contact but may involve reducing the frequency or intensity of interactions. Creating boundaries around the time and energy you invest in the relationship can help protect your own well-being while maintaining a connection.

Forgiveness and patience are key aspects of managing difficult family members. It can be challenging to let go of past grievances or hurtful behaviors, but holding onto them can perpetuate conflict and strain the relationship further. Forgiveness does not mean condoning or excusing hurtful actions, but rather it is a way of releasing the emotional burden and freeing yourself from the past. Patience is essential because changing deeply ingrained behaviors or dynamics within a family takes time, and progress may be slow.

In conclusion, managing difficult family members is a complex and emotionally challenging endeavor, but it is essential for maintaining family bonds and personal well-being. Effective communication, setting boundaries, practicing empathy, seeking outside support, self-care, creating distance when necessary, forgiveness, and patience are all valuable strategies for dealing with challenging family dynamics. While there is no one-size-fits-all approach, combining these strategies can help individuals navigate their relationships with difficult family members more effectively and ultimately foster healthier and more harmonious family connections. Remember that managing difficult family members is a process that requires ongoing effort and a commitment to the well-being of both yourself and your family.

Dealing with challenging friends or acquaintances

Friendships and acquaintanceships can bring joy, companionship, and support into our lives, but they can also come with challenges. Interactions with challenging friends or acquaintances can be emotionally taxing, as these individuals may exhibit behaviors such as unreliability, negativity, manipulation, or constant drama. Navigating these relationships can be complex, as they often occupy a unique space between the intimacy of family and the formality of professional relationships. This section explores strategies for dealing with challenging friends or acquaintances, focusing on communication, setting boundaries, empathy, self-care, and the possibility of reevaluation.

Effective communication is essential when interacting with difficult friends or acquaintances. Open and honest dialogue can help address issues, clarify misunderstandings, and improve the overall dynamic. If a friend or acquaintance is exhibiting behaviors that trouble you, it's important to express your feelings and concerns calmly and assertively. Choose a suitable time and place to have the conversation, and use "I" statements to express your perspective and emotions. For instance, you might say, "I've noticed that our interactions often involve drama, and it makes me feel drained. I'd like us to find a way to have more positive interactions." By addressing the problem directly and respectfully, you create an opportunity for positive change.

Setting boundaries is a key strategy for managing challenging friendships or acquaintanceships. Communicate your expectations clearly for respectful behavior and assertively express your own needs and limits. Challenging individuals may push boundaries, so it's important to reinforce them consistently. Be prepared for resistance or pushback, as they may not react positively to boundaries, but maintaining them is crucial for your own well-being. Setting boundaries can help develop a more balanced and manageable relationship.

Empathy is a powerful tool for dealing with challenging friends or acquaintances. Try to understand their perspective and motivations, even if their behavior frustrates you. Challenging individuals may have their own struggles, insecurities, or unmet needs that drive their behavior. By showing empathy, you can foster a more compassionate understanding of their actions, which can lead to improved communication and potentially a more positive relationship.

Self-care is essential when dealing with challenging friends or acquaintances. Interacting with individuals who drain your energy or create stress can be emotionally exhausting. Prioritize your own well-being by participating in self-care practices that promote emotional resilience, such as mindfulness, exercise, meditation, or seeking support from other friends or professionals. Maintaining your emotional health is vital when dealing with challenging relationships.

Sometimes, it may be necessary to reevaluate the relationship itself. Consider whether the friendship or acquaintanceship is overall positive and beneficial to your life. While it's natural for relationships to have ups and downs, if a relationship consistently brings more distress than joy, it may be worth considering whether it's worth maintaining. Assess whether the relationship aligns with your values, supports your growth, and contributes positively to your life. It's important to remember that you have the agency to choose the relationships that are most conducive to your well-being.

In some cases, seeking outside support or guidance can be valuable when dealing with challenging friends or acquaintances. Confiding in a trusted family member or a trusted friend can provide emotional validation and perspective. They may offer insights or advice on how to navigate the relationship more effectively. Additionally, asking the guidance of a therapist or counselor can provide a secure and neutral space to explore your feelings, options, and strategies for managing challenging relationships. Therapy can also help you establish coping skills and explore the emotional challenges that arise in such interactions.

Ultimately, dealing with challenging friends or acquaintances requires a combination of strategies, including effective communication, boundary-setting, empathy, self-care, and, when necessary, reevaluation. While it can be difficult to navigate these relationships, remember that you have the power to control your responses and choices when it comes to maintaining or letting go of friendships or acquaintanceships. Your well-being and emotional health should always be a priority, and it's okay to make decisions that support your own happiness and growth.

Maintaining healthy personal relationships

Healthy personal relationships are essential for our emotional well-being and overall quality of life. Whether they are with friends, romantic partners, family members, or colleagues, these relationships provide support, companionship, and a sense of belonging. However, nurturing and sustaining healthy personal relationships is not always easy and often requires effort, communication, and understanding. This section explores key strategies and principles for maintaining healthy personal relationships, emphasizing communication, trust, boundaries, empathy, and self-care.

Effective communication is the bedrock of every healthy personal relationship. Open and honest dialogue helps build trust, resolve conflicts, and foster understanding between individuals. It involves not only expressing one's thoughts and feelings but also actively listening to others. Active listening means providing the speaker your full attention, showing empathy, and seeking to comprehend their perspective. When disagreements or conflicts arise, addressing them calmly and assertively can lead to resolution and strengthened bonds. Encouraging open communication and creating a secure space for honest conversations is essential for maintaining healthy relationships.

Trust is a fundamental element of healthy personal relationships. It is built over time through consistency, reliability, and integrity. Trust involves having confidence in the other person's honesty, intentions, and commitment. To maintain trust, it is important to keep promises, be dependable, and communicate openly. Trust can be fragile and easily eroded by dishonesty or betrayal, so it must be valued and protected in any relationship.

Setting and respecting boundaries is crucial for maintaining healthy personal relationships. Boundaries is known as the limits of acceptable behavior and help individuals feel safe and respected within the relationship. Communicating boundaries assertively is essential to ensure that both parties understand as well as respect each other's needs and limits. When boundaries are crossed or violated, addressing the issue promptly and assertively is necessary to maintain the integrity of the relationship.

Empathy is a vital component of healthy personal relationships. It entails understanding as well as sharing the emotions of others, even when they differ from our own. Empathy fosters compassion, connection, and a deeper understanding of the other person's experiences and feelings. It is important to actively practice empathy by listening attentively, validating emotions, and seeking to understand the perspectives of others. Empathy can help navigate conflicts with sensitivity and build emotional intimacy in relationships.

Self-care plays a significant role in maintaining healthy personal relationships. Caring for one's physical, emotional, and mental well-being ensures that individuals bring their best selves to their relationships. When individuals prioritize self-care, they are better equipped to handle stress, manage emotions, and contribute positively to their relationships. Self-care practices can include exercise, mindfulness, relaxation techniques, seeking support from friends or professionals, and participating in activities that bring joy and fulfillment.

Forgiveness is an important aspect of maintaining healthy personal relationships. No relationship is without its challenges, and conflicts or misunderstandings can arise. Forgiveness entails letting go of resentment, anger, or hurt feelings and selecting to move forward with a clean slate. Forgiveness does not mean condoning hurtful actions but rather freeing oneself from the emotional burden of the past. It allows relationships to heal and grow stronger, provided that both parties are committed to positive change.

Spending quality time together is necessary for maintaining healthy personal relationships. Shared experiences, meaningful conversations, and creating memories together help strengthen the emotional bonds between individuals. Making an effort to prioritize time for each other, whether through regular date nights, family outings, or quality conversations, can contribute to a more fulfilling and connected relationship.

Flexibility and adaptability are key principles for maintaining healthy personal relationships. Individuals change and grow over time, and so do their needs and priorities. Being willing to adapt to these changes and accommodate each other's evolving goals and aspirations can help maintain harmony and longevity in relationships. Flexibility also means being open to compromise and finding mutually beneficial solutions when conflicts or differences arise.

Supporting each other's individual growth and personal development is essential for maintaining healthy personal relationships. While it's important to share experiences and connect, it's equally important to recognize and support each other's individual pursuits, passions, and goals. Encouraging personal growth and celebrating each other's achievements and milestones can enhance the relationship and foster a sense of empowerment and fulfillment.

In conclusion, maintaining healthy personal relationships is a lifelong journey that requires effort, communication, and a commitment to growth and understanding. Effective communication, trust, boundaries, empathy, self-care, forgiveness, quality time, flexibility, adaptability, and support for individual growth are key principles for nurturing and sustaining healthy relationships. While challenges and conflicts may arise, the willingness to address them openly and with empathy can lead to resolution and growth. Healthy personal relationships enrich our lives, providing us with support, love, and a sense of belonging, making them a valuable and worthwhile endeavor.

CHAPTER X

Cultivating Patience and Resilience

The role of patience in peaceful coexistence

Patience is a virtue frequently overlooked in our fast- paced and increasingly interconnected world. Yet, it plays a fundamental role in promoting peaceful coexistence among individuals, communities, and nations. Patience involves the ability to remain calm and composed in the face of adversity, to tolerate differences, and to persevere in the pursuit of understanding and compromise. In a world characterized by diversity and complexity, patience is a powerful tool for resolving conflicts, fostering empathy, and building harmonious relationships. This section explores the multifaceted role of patience in peaceful coexistence, emphasizing its significance in conflict resolution, empathy cultivation, and the development of tolerant and compassionate societies.

Conflict resolution is a primary arena where patience shines in promoting peaceful coexistence. Conflicts are inevitable in human interaction, arising from differences in perspectives, interests, values, and needs. In such situations, patience acts as a buffer against impulsive reactions and escalations. Rather than resorting to anger or aggression, patient individuals are more likely to participate in constructive dialogue, seeking to understand the underlying causes of the conflict and working toward mutually acceptable solutions. Patience allows space for de-escalation, negotiation, and compromise, ultimately leading to resolutions addressing all parties' concerns.

Furthermore, patience is closely linked to empathy, a fundamental quality for peaceful coexistence. Empathy entails the capacity to understand and share the emotions and perspectives of others. It requires patience to listen attentively, withhold judgment, and allow others to express themselves fully. In practicing empathy, patient individuals develop a deeper understanding of the experiences, motivations, and struggles of those around them. This understanding, in turn, fosters compassion and tolerance, as individuals recognize the common humanity that unites us despite our differences. In a world marked by various cultures, beliefs, and backgrounds, empathy driven by patience bridges divides and promotes unity.

Patience is also a cornerstone for building tolerant and compassionate societies. In today's globalized world, societies are increasingly diverse, bringing together individuals from varied cultures, backgrounds, and belief systems. Tolerance and coexistence in such societies demand patience in acknowledging and respecting differences. Patient individuals are more willing to engage in dialogue with those who hold opposing views, recognizing that change and understanding often require time. They are less prone to prejudgments or biases and more open to the possibility of growth and transformation in themselves and others. A patient society values diversity as a source of strength and embraces the idea that peaceful coexistence is rooted in acceptance and inclusion.

In addition to interpersonal relationships, patience plays a significant role in international diplomacy and global peacekeeping efforts. The patience of diplomats and negotiators is often tested in complex and protracted conflicts where the stakes are high. These individuals must engage in lengthy and challenging negotiations, often with parties who hold deeply entrenched positions. Patience enables diplomats to maintain a diplomatic and constructive tone, despite setbacks or delays. It allows them to persevere in seeking common ground and working toward lasting peace agreements. The role of patience in international relations extends to conflict prevention and crisis management, where it serves to de- escalate tensions and facilitate dialogue between nations.

However, patience is not synonymous with passivity or complacency. It does not mean tolerating injustice, oppression, or harm to oneself or others. Instead, patience empowers individuals and societies to pursue justice and change through non-violent means. Patient activism involves persistent and determined efforts to address social injustices and promote positive change. This type of patience is exemplified by figures like Mahatma Gandhi and also Martin Luther King Jr., who advocated for civil rights and social justice through peaceful means.

Moreover, patience complements other virtues that contribute to peaceful coexistence, such as forgiveness and reconciliation. In situations where harm has occurred or trust has been broken, patience is a key ingredient in the process of healing and rebuilding relationships. It allows individuals and communities to approach forgiveness and reconciliation with empathy and a willingness to move forward, even when the path is difficult and painful.

In conclusion, patience is a vital and multifaceted virtue that plays a central role in peaceful coexistence at various levels, from interpersonal relationships to international diplomacy. It serves as a linchpin for conflict resolution, empathy cultivation, and the development of tolerant and compassionate societies. In a world marked by diversity, complexity, and adversity, patience offers a path to understanding, tolerance, and unity. As individuals and as societies, we must recognize and nurture the value of patience to foster peaceful coexistence and build a better world.

Strategies for building resilience

The ability to overcome hardship, adjust to difficult circumstances, and preserve mental and emotional health in the face of stress or trauma is referred to as resilience. It is a quality that can be developed and strengthened over time, enabling individuals to better navigate life's ups and downs. Building resilience is essential for not only coping with difficult circumstances but also thriving and growing as a result of them. This section explores strategies for building resilience, emphasizing the importance of social support, positive thinking, self-care, problem-solving skills, and finding purpose and meaning in life.

One of the critical strategies for building resilience is cultivating a strong support network. Social support is a crucial buffer against stress and adversity. Friends, family, and trusted individuals can provide emotional support, a listening ear, and guidance during challenging times. Building and keeping meaningful relationships with others is essential for resilience, as it fosters a sense of belonging and connectedness, reinforcing the belief that one is not alone in facing difficulties.

Positive thinking and optimism are key components of resilience. Optimistic individuals tend to have a more constructive outlook on life and are better equipped to handle setbacks. Positive thinking involves reframing negative thoughts and focusing on opportunities for growth and learning in adversity. It does not mean denying the reality of challenging situations but rather approaching them with a mindset that emphasizes resilience and the potential for positive outcomes.

Self-care is a crucial strategy for building and maintaining resilience. It involves taking deliberate steps to prioritize one's physical, emotional, and mental well-being. Self- care practices can include regular exercise, a balanced diet, adequate sleep, relaxation techniques, mindfulness, and seeking support from professionals or support groups. By investing in self-care, individuals can better cope with stress, maintain emotional stability, and develop the capacity to face challenges with greater resilience.

Problem-solving skills are essential for resilience, as they enable individuals to approach difficulties in a systematic and constructive manner. Effective problem-solving involves identifying the problem, generating potential solutions, evaluating the advantages as well as disadvantages of each solution, and implementing the most suitable course of action. Developing problem-solving skills not only enhances one's ability to navigate challenges but also boosts self-confidence and self-efficacy.

Another vital aspect of building resilience is finding purpose and meaning in life. Having a sense of purpose provides a source of motivation and resilience during difficult times. Individuals who feel a sense of purpose are more likely to persevere and also bounce back from setbacks because they are driven by a deeper sense of meaning beyond the immediate challenges they face. Purpose can be found in various forms, such as meaningful work, family, community involvement, or personal passions and interests.

Adaptive coping strategies are essential for resilience. Coping involves the strategies and mechanisms individuals use to manage stress and adversity. Adaptive coping strategies are those that promote well-being and resilience rather than exacerbating stress. Examples of adaptive coping strategies include seeking social support, practicing relaxation techniques, engaging in problem-solving, and maintaining a positive outlook. Developing and employing effective coping strategies is crucial for building resilience in the face of life's challenges.

Resilience can also be nurtured through the practice of mindfulness and emotional regulation. Mindfulness involves being present in the moment, accepting one's thoughts and feelings without judgment, and promoting a sense of inner calm and clarity. This practice allows individuals to respond to stressors in a balanced and composed manner, rather than reacting impulsively. Emotional regulation skills help individuals manage and navigate intense emotions, preventing them from becoming overwhelming or destructive.

Additionally, fostering a sense of gratitude and practicing acts of kindness can enhance resilience. Gratitude entails recognizing as well as appreciating the positive aspects of life, even in the midst of difficulties. It can improve overall well-being and provide a sense of perspective that helps individuals cope with adversity. Acts of kindness, both giving and receiving, can strengthen social interactions and contribute to a sense of purpose and meaning, further enhancing resilience.

Lastly, building resilience requires acknowledging that setbacks and challenges are a natural part of life. Resilience is not about avoiding adversity but rather about facing it with courage and a sense of empowerment. It involves learning from failures and setbacks, using them as opportunities for growth and personal development. Embracing a mindset of resilience means recognizing that challenges are a part of the human experience and that they can be catalysts for strength and transformation.

In conclusion, building resilience is a lifelong journey that involves the cultivation of social support, positive thinking, self-care, problem-solving skills, a sense of purpose and meaning, adaptive coping strategies, mindfulness, emotional regulation, gratitude, and acts of kindness. Resilience enables individuals not only to weather life's storms but also to emerge from them stronger and more capable. It is a quality that can be developed and honed through practice and self-awareness, ultimately leading to a more resilient and empowered approach to life's challenges. Remember that resilience is not the absence of difficulties but rather the ability to thrive in spite of them.

Staying committed to personal growth

Personal growth is a lifelong journey that entails continuous self-improvement, development, and the pursuit of one's full potential. It encompasses various aspects of our lives, including our physical, emotional, intellectual, and spiritual well-being. While the concept of personal growth may sound appealing, it requires commitment, dedication, and persistence to truly make progress. In this section, we will explore the importance of staying committed to personal growth and discuss some strategies that can help individuals on this transformative journey.

First and foremost, personal growth is essential for achieving a fulfilling and meaningful life. It permits individuals to discover their strengths and weaknesses, set meaningful goals, and work towards becoming the best version of themselves. Without a commitment to personal growth, people may remain stagnant, missing out on valuable opportunities for self-discovery and improvement. In essence, personal growth is not a destination but a continuous process, and those who commit to it are more likely to lead happier and more successful lives.

One of the key reasons for staying committed to personal growth is that it empowers individuals to overcome obstacles and challenges. Life is full of ups and downs, and personal growth equips us with the resilience and skills needed to navigate through difficult times. When we are committed to our personal development, we become more adaptable and better equipped to handle adversity. This resilience can make a great difference in how we perceive and respond to life's challenges.

Furthermore, personal growth is closely related to self-awareness. It involves reflecting on our thoughts, behaviors, and beliefs, which in turn helps us gain a deeper understanding of ourselves. This self-awareness is a valuable tool for personal development, as it enables us to identify areas in which we need to improve and make conscious choices to change and grow. Without commitment to personal growth, many individuals may remain unaware of their limitations and, as a result, miss out on opportunities for self-improvement.

Moreover, staying committed to personal growth can enhance our relationships with others. As we grow and evolve, we become better at understanding and empathizing with the people around us. We develop better communication skills, become more patient, and learn to appreciate the diversity of perspectives and experiences. This, in turn, leads to stronger and more fulfilling relationships, both personally and professionally. Personal growth can also help us break free from negative patterns and the habits that may have hindered our relationships in the past.

In addition to personal relationships, a commitment to personal growth can also lead to professional success. Many employers value employees who are dedicated to self-improvement and continuous learning. Individuals who invest in their personal development are often more adaptable, innovative, and motivated in the workplace. They are more likely to take on new challenges, pursue additional training, and seek opportunities for career advancement. In a quickly changing world, the ability to adapt and grow is a valuable asset in any career.

While the benefits of personal growth are clear, staying committed to it can be challenging. Life is busy, and there are numerous distractions and obstacles that can get in the way. However, there are strategies that individuals can utilize to maintain their commitment to personal growth.

One effective strategy is goal setting. Setting specific, achievable goals can provide individuals with a sense of direction and purpose on their personal growth journey. These objectives can be short- or long-term, and they should be challenging yet attainable. By regularly reviewing and adjusting their goals, individuals can stay motivated and track their progress.

Another important strategy is self-discipline. Personal growth requires consistent effort and dedication. It often entails stepping out of one's comfort zone and facing challenges head-on. Developing self-discipline is crucial for staying committed to personal growth, as it helps individuals overcome procrastination and maintain focus on their goals.

Moreover, seeking support and guidance from others can be immensely beneficial. This can involve finding a mentor or coach who can provide guidance and accountability. It can also mean connecting with a community of like-minded individuals who share similar personal growth goals. The support and encouragement of others can be a potent motivator and can help individuals stay committed to their journey of self-improvement.

In conclusion, staying committed to personal growth is essential for leading a fulfilling and a successful life. It empowers individuals to overcome challenges, enhances self-awareness, improves relationships, and contributes to professional success. While it may require effort and dedication, the benefits of personal growth are well worth the investment. By setting goals, practicing self-discipline, and seeking support from others, individuals can stay committed to their personal growth journey and continue to evolve and develop throughout their lives. Ultimately, personal growth is not just a choice; it is a lifelong commitment to becoming the best version of oneself.

Chapter XI

Real-Life Success Stories

Interviews or case studies of individuals who successfully mastered dealing with difficult people

Dealing with difficult people is a universal challenge that many individuals encounter in various aspects of life, from the workplace to personal relationships. Successfully navigating these interactions requires a combination of interpersonal skills, emotional intelligence, and resilience. While there is no one-size-fits-all approach to handling difficult people, it can be instructive to examine the experiences of individuals who have successfully mastered this skill. In this section, we will explore interviews and case studies of such individuals to gain insights into their strategies, mindset, and techniques for effectively managing difficult people.

One common scenario where individuals frequently encounter difficult people is in the workplace. A prime example of someone who has mastered dealing with difficult colleagues is Sarah, a seasoned project manager in a large corporation. Sarah recalls a time when she had to work closely with a colleague named David, known for his abrasive and confrontational communication style. Instead of reacting to his behavior with frustration or anger, Sarah chose to approach the situation with curiosity and empathy. She initiated a one-on-one conversation with David to understand his motivations and concerns better. During the conversation, she discovered that David was feeling overwhelmed and stressed due to high workload and tight deadlines.

Sarah's approach was rooted in empathy, and she realized that addressing the underlying issue – David's stress – would be more effective than reacting to his abrasive behavior. She offered her support and assistance in managing his workload and suggested collaborating on a plan to meet deadlines more effectively. By taking this approach, Sarah not only diffused the tension between them but also helped David improve his communication and teamwork skills over time. Her ability to remain calm, empathetic, and solution-focused was instrumental in mastering the art of dealing with difficult colleagues.

In personal relationships, dealing with difficult family members can be particularly challenging. One individual who exemplifies mastery in this area is Michael, who had a strained relationship with his older brother, John. John had a history of addiction and erratic behavior, which often caused turmoil within the family. Instead of cutting ties or reacting with anger, Michael chose a different path. He recognized that addiction was a complex issue and that John needed support rather than judgment.

Michael took the initiative to educate himself about addiction and its impact on families. He attended support groups and counseling sessions to better understand how to communicate effectively with his brother. Instead of enabling John's behavior, he set clear boundaries and offered his support for addiction treatment. Michael's journey involved immense patience and empathy, as it took years for John to fully commit to recovery. However, through Michael's unwavering support and willingness to maintain boundaries, their relationship eventually transformed into a healthier and more supportive one. His case illustrates the power of patience, empathy, and setting boundaries in dealing with difficult family members.

In the realm of personal relationships, romantic partnerships can also present challenges when dealing with difficult individuals. One such case is the story of Lisa, who was in a relationship with Alex, someone with a history of emotional volatility and mood swings. Instead of reacting defensively or withdrawing from the relationship, Lisa chose to engage in open and honest communication. She initiated a conversation with Alex to express her concerns about his behavior and its impact on their relationship.

Lisa's approach was marked by assertiveness and empathy. She acknowledged Alex's struggles with managing his emotions and encouraged him to seek professional help. She also set clear boundaries, emphasizing the importance of respectful and healthy communication in their relationship. Over time, Alex recognized the value of her feedback and took steps to address his emotional challenges. Their relationship improved as a result of Lisa's courage to address difficult issues head-on and her commitment to fostering a healthier partnership.

In some cases, individuals encounter difficult people outside of work and personal relationships, such as in community or volunteer settings. Emma, an active volunteer in her local community, faced the challenge of dealing with a particularly demanding and critical community member named Robert. Robert had a reputation for micromanaging projects and constantly finding fault with others' efforts. Emma decided to take a diplomatic approach.

She invited Robert for a one-on-one meeting to discuss his concerns and suggestions for improvement. During their conversation, she actively listened to his feedback and acknowledged his contributions to the community. Emma also demonstrated flexibility by incorporating some of Robert's suggestions into their projects. By doing so, she not only diffused his confrontational attitude but also turned him into a more constructive and collaborative team member. Emma's ability to engage with empathy, diplomacy, and openness to feedback played a crucial role in mastering the challenge of dealing with difficult individuals in community settings.

In summary, interviews and case studies of individuals who have successfully mastered the art of dealing with difficult people offer valuable insights and strategies. These individuals demonstrate the importance of empathy, patience, clear communication, and setting boundaries in effectively managing challenging interactions. Whether in the workplace, personal relationships, or community settings, the stories of these individuals provide inspiration and guidance for those seeking to enhance their own skills in dealing with difficult people. Their experiences underscore the idea that, with the right approach and mindset, individuals can transform challenging relationships into opportunities for growth and improved connections.

CHAPTER XII

Tools and Resources

Books, courses, and resources for further learning

In our personal and professional lives, we often encounter difficult people. These individuals can present challenges ranging from communication issues and personality clashes to conflicts and stress. However, learning how to effectively deal with difficult people is a valuable skill that can lead to better relationships, reduced stress, and improved overall well-being. Fortunately, there are various resources available, including books, courses, and online platforms, that provide valuable insights and strategies for handling such situations. In this section, we will explore some of the best resources for further learning in dealing with difficult people.

Books have long been a source of knowledge and guidance, and they continue to offer valuable insights into understanding and managing difficult individuals. One highly recommended book on this topic is "Difficult Conversations: How to Discuss What Matters Most" by Douglas Stone, Bruce Patton, and Sheila Heen. This book provides a framework for approaching tough conversations and offers practical advice on improving communication and resolving conflicts.

Another insightful book is "Crucial Conversations: Tools for Talking When Stakes Are High" by Al Switzler, Joseph Grenny, and Ron McMillan. This resource focuses on how to handle high-stakes conversations effectively, offering strategies for navigating difficult discussions with confidence and empathy.

For those interested in a comprehensive guide to dealing with difficult people, "The Emotionally Intelligent Manager" by David R. Caruso and Peter Salovey is a valuable resource. This book explores the idea of emotional intelligence and provides practical techniques for managing emotions and relationships, which is essential in dealing with challenging individuals.

Courses and workshops can also be excellent resources for learning how to handle difficult people. Many universities, online platforms, and professional development organizations offer courses on interpersonal skills and conflict resolution. One notable course available on platforms like Coursera and LinkedIn Learning is "Managing Conflict" by the University of California, Irvine. This course covers conflict resolution strategies, negotiation techniques, and effective communication skills, all of which are crucial when dealing with difficult people.

Another worthwhile option is "Dealing with Difficult People" by Dale Carnegie Training. This course focuses specifically on understanding and managing challenging individuals in various situations, both personally and professionally. Participants learn practical strategies for diffusing conflicts and improving relationships.

In addition to books and courses, online resources and communities provide valuable insights and support for individuals looking to enhance their skills in dealing with difficult people. Websites like Psychology Today and Verywell Mind offer articles, tips, and expert advice on handling challenging personalities and improving interpersonal relationships.

Online forums as well as discussion boards can also be valuable resources for seeking advice and sharing experiences with others who are dealing with same challenges. Websites like Reddit and Quora have dedicated sections where users can ask questions and also participate in discussions related to difficult people and conflict resolution.

Furthermore, podcasts have become a popular medium for self-improvement and personal development. Several podcasts focus on topics related to interpersonal skills and dealing with difficult people. "The Art of Charm," for instance, offers insights into social dynamics, communication, and building rapport, which can be valuable when dealing with challenging individuals.

When it comes to online communities, LinkedIn and Facebook groups dedicated to personal development and interpersonal skills are excellent places to connect with like-minded individuals, share experiences, and learn from others' perspectives. These groups often feature discussions, webinars, and resources related to dealing with difficult people.

In conclusion, dealing with difficult people is a skill that can greatly enhance both personal and professional relationships. Books, courses, and online resources offer valuable insights and strategies for effectively managing challenging individuals. Whether you prefer to delve into books for in-depth knowledge, enroll in courses for structured learning, or engage with online communities for shared experiences, there are numerous resources available to help you develop the skills needed to navigate challenging interactions with confidence and empathy. By investing in further learning, you can improve your ability to handle difficult people and create more positive and productive relationships in all aspects of your life.

Creating a personal action plan for peaceful coexistence

In a world marked by diversity, conflict, and differing perspectives, the aspiration for peaceful coexistence is of utmost importance. Whether in our communities, workplaces, or personal relationships, the ability to foster harmony and understanding among individuals of varying backgrounds and beliefs is a vital skill. To achieve peaceful coexistence, it is essential to develop a personal action plan that promotes tolerance, empathy, and open communication. This section will navigate the key components of creating a personal action plan for peaceful coexistence and its significance in fostering a more harmonious world.

The first step in crafting a personal action plan for peaceful coexistence is self-awareness. Understanding our own biases, prejudices, and beliefs is crucial. We must acknowledge that we, too, hold certain assumptions and stereotypes that can impact our interactions with others. Self-reflection allows us to identify areas where we may need to grow and change. It is necessary to confront our own biases and actively work to challenge and overcome them. By recognizing our own biases, we can become more open-minded and empathetic, setting the stage for more peaceful interactions with others.

Empathy is a cornerstone of peaceful coexistence. It entails putting ourselves in the shoes of others, striving to understand their feelings, perspectives, and experiences. To develop empathy, we should actively listen to others without judgment and be genuinely interested in their stories and viewpoints. Empathy permits us to connect on a deeper level and build bridges of understanding. It helps us see beyond our differences and recognize the humanity that unites us all.

Effective communication is another vital element of a personal action plan for peaceful coexistence. Open, respectful, and honest communication is essential for resolving conflicts, addressing misunderstandings, and building trust. We should strive to communicate our thoughts and feelings clearly and actively seek feedback from others. It is important to be aware of our tone, body language, and the impact of our words. By promoting an environment of open communication, we can create spaces where individuals feel safe sharing their thoughts and concerns.

Respect for diversity is a fundamental principle of peaceful coexistence. We should celebrate and embrace the rich tapestry of cultures, backgrounds, and beliefs that make up our global community. Rather than viewing differences as a source of conflict, we should see them as an opportunity for learning and growth. Respect for diversity means valuing the contributions and perspectives of all individuals, irrespective of their background, and promoting inclusion and equality for everyone.

Conflict resolution skills are essential in any personal action plan for peaceful coexistence. Conflicts are a natural part of human interactions, but how we approach and resolve them can make a significant difference. It is crucial to address conflicts constructively, focusing on finding solutions rather than assigning blame. Effective conflict resolution involves active listening, compromise, and a willingness to understand the underlying issues. By approaching conflicts with a problem-solving mindset, we can change them into opportunities for growth and stronger relationships.

Promoting education and awareness is another key aspect of a personal action plan for peaceful coexistence. Educating ourselves and others about different cultures, religions, and perspectives can help break down stereotypes and reduce prejudice. We should actively seek out opportunities to learn from diverse sources, such as books, documentaries, and cultural events. Additionally, we can engage in dialogue with people from different backgrounds to gain a more profound understanding of their experiences and viewpoints.

Taking action in our communities and beyond is an integral part of a personal action plan for peaceful coexistence. We should actively seek opportunities to contribute to positive change. This may involve volunteering with organizations that promote tolerance and inclusion, participating in community initiatives, or advocating for policies that promote equality and diversity. By taking concrete actions, we can make a tangible impact on creating more inclusive and harmonious environments.

Self-reflection and continuous improvement are essential in maintaining a personal action plan for peaceful coexistence. We should regularly assess our progress, celebrate our successes, and identify areas where we can further grow. It is important to recognize that promoting peaceful coexistence is an ongoing journey that requires dedication and effort. By staying committed to our personal action plan, we can contribute to a more peaceful and united world.

In conclusion, creating a personal action plan for peaceful coexistence is a meaningful and necessary endeavor. It requires self-awareness, empathy, effective communication, respect for diversity, conflict resolution skills, education, and active engagement in our communities. By embracing these principles and taking concrete actions, we can make a positive impact on the world around us. Peaceful coexistence is not merely an ideal; it is a tangible goal that each of us can work toward, ultimately leading to a more harmonious and compassionate society.

CONCLUSION

In the journey through "Peaceful Coexistence: Mastering the Skill of Dealing with Difficult People," we have explored the intricate dynamics of human interaction and conflict resolution. This book has been a guide, offering invaluable insights into understanding the complexities of dealing with challenging individuals, whether in personal relationships, the workplace, or broader social contexts.

Throughout these pages, we have delved into the nature of difficult personalities, the impact they can have on our lives, and the strategies for managing such interactions effectively. We've learned that empathy, active listening, and self-awareness are the cornerstones of peaceful coexistence. By embracing these principles, we can foster understanding, build bridges, and find common ground even in the most trying circumstances.

As we conclude this journey, it is essential to remember that mastering the skill of dealing with difficult people is an ongoing process. It demands patience, practice, and a commitment to personal growth. Each encounter with a challenging individual is an opportunity to apply the knowledge and techniques discussed in this book, gradually honing our abilities to navigate complex interactions with grace and wisdom.

Ultimately, "Peaceful Coexistence" empowers us to transform conflicts into opportunities for connection and personal development. By approaching difficult people with empathy and self-awareness, we not only enhance our own well-being but also participate to a more harmonious and understanding world. May the lessons learned within these pages serve as a compass, guiding you toward a future filled with peaceful coexistence and enriched relationships.

Thank you for buying and reading/ listening to our book. If you found this book useful/ helpful please take a few minutes and leave a review on the platform where you purchased our book. Your feedback matters greatly to us.